LETTERS HOME FROM SEA

LETTERS HOME FROM SEA

The Life and Letters of
Solon J. Hanson
Down East Sailor

L. J. Webster *&* M. A. Noah

HOBBLEBUSH

ISBN 13: 978-0-9760896-5-0
ISBN 10: 0-9760896-5-3
Library of Congress Control Number: 2006924598

Designed and composed in Adobe Garamond Pro
at Hobblebush Books,
Brookline, New Hampshire

Printed in the United States of America

Line drawings by Lucy Jane Webster

Published by:

Hobblebush Books

17-A Old Milford Road
Brookline, New Hampshire 03033

www.hobblebush.com

*This book is dedicated to those who love
the adventure of going to sea.*

Contents

Preface

OUR ANCESTORS OF THE Castine-Penobscot Maine region were long associated with the sea. They fished and farmed; developed and defended; and wrote letters and diaries that still speak to us today. This book relates the experiences of Solon J. Hanson through his letters home and his personal diary.* The letters were written in the beautiful script of the mid-19th century, the aged ink beginning to fade. Solon's words expressed a young man's desire to accompany his father to sea and then the excitement of his adventures at sea. He accepted the challenges vigorously and optimistically. The letters tell of the seaman's life and report locations of ships and people of the mid 1800s.

We have chosen to publish the letters verbatim to preserve Solon's style, which includes: a lack of capitalization and punctuation, errant spellings, and idiomatic expressions peculiar to his time. We elected not to embellish material we could not document. Gaps in continuity remain open to the imagination.

Working with the letters to publish the book has been an education for us. Little did I realize, in 1976, the extent of the project I had accepted when my mother handed me photocopies of the letters and asked that they be organized and published. I am a visual artist and Meg Noah, my daughter, is an accomplished computer programmer, thus able to put all the material into a format for publishing. We started with the letters first, thinking we would publish them directly. Then, as we reread them, we discovered unfamiliar and obsolete terms and that triggered a larger

---

* Hanson's niece, Helen Peterson Conner, daughter of his sister Lucy Jane, had kept these. After Helen's death, her sister-in-law Vivian Kenniston Conner retained the material. The letters came to our attention in the 1970s when Vivian K. Conner's daughters, my mother, Marian Helen Conner Myers, and her sister, Virginia Conner Moseley, were examining papers left in her Castine house.

book to help readers better understand the content and context of the writings.

Also recorded is Solon's diary, a treasure that surfaced when I was going through the papers again in the summer of 1996. I was looking for the daguerreotype.* Solon had referred to and came across a farm-ledger book his father was keeping. As I scanned the book, I was surprised to discover neatly written pages, day by day, of Solon's voyage. I cannot begin to express how I felt at that moment. To think of the journey this little book had made and here it was in my hands. I was overwhelmed. It had been over 25 years since my mother had handed me the copies. At that time she knew I could not start immediately on her request. Now we wish she had known the diary was there, hidden within the papers.

It is now 2006. Meg has been a great help encouraging and working with this book. We have learned to write and rewrite, and then to delete extraneous material. We have relished reading other author's accounts of the great age of sail in the 1800s. Studying Solon's letters today moves me, as it did when we first discovered the fragile collection years ago.

—Lucy Jane Myers Webster

---

* A daguerreotype is a photograph made by exposing an image on a light-sensitive silver-coated metallic plate.

Acknowledgments

MEG AND I THANK the many people who patiently contributed insight into the history of cod fishing, New England life in the 1800s, and the writing of this book.

One morning while at Bah's, Castine's Bake House and local breakfast haunt, Phil Perkins, retired history teacher (died, 1997), enlightened our understanding of trade in the 1800s, particularly with goods to Russia in the mid-19th century. He also told of his encounters with the wonderful sweets in Herman Echenagucia's Castine bakery.

We appreciate the format suggestions from Ellenore Doudiet, former director of the Wilson Museum (who died in 2004), and Patricia Hutchins, curator and director of the Wilson Museum, and John G. Arrison, a librarian at the Penobscot Marine Museum in Searsport Maine. Correspondence with Mr. Edward Ives of the Maine Folklife Center at the University of Maine added information about the Hanson family, and Genevieve Dawson, Graduate Assistant Special Collections, of the University of Missouri-Columbia Ellis Library, kindly assisted finding 1858 newspaper articles. We thank Jose and Doris Albernaz and Paul Blake for the translation of the non-English letter sent to Lucy Jane Hanson Echenagucia Peterson.

Albert E. Myers explained the importance of indexing and we have referenced his genealogical research. Howard W. Myers explained the joys of sailing.

In particular, we thank Sidney Hall for his professional services above and beyond. We thank Mona and Wolfgang Bode for reading our original text and suggesting that we develop it further. We thank the Brookline New Hampshire Book Club, in particular Jen Vertullo and Carmen Yarusso, for reading and providing valuable feedback. Carol Block and Jennifer B. Webster added insight into publishing and encouraged us when we needed it most.

Many of my artist friends provided precious moral support. We have learned from the material we searched and read.

We are grateful to our husbands, John Blair Webster and Paul V. Noah for their patience and support. We especially appreciate Marian Conner Myers and Virginia Conner Moseley for the legacy of the letters and requesting that they be published eventually.

—*Lucy Jane Myers Webster*

LETTERS HOME FROM SEA

CHEERFULNESS.

Prologue

THE COMMERCIAL CENTER of Castine, Maine is where Main Street and Water Street meet. Here two favorite breakfast spots, Bah's Bake House and The Variety, fill with townspeople, summer folk, and tourists to exchange news, solve problems, and nurture friendships. We return annually as summer folk, yet we return to our heritage. For generations, this meeting ground has continued for finding out what was and is happening in the lives of the townspeople and friends, whether at home or at sea. We know our ancestors convened on this same spot. Herman Echenagucia had a bakery on the land in front of Bah's. Helen Peterson Conner ran a boarding house for a few years in the building of the present day Water Witch.

Here in 1629, Plymouth Colony set up a coastal trading outpost to acquire the furs needed to fulfill their contract with the Merchant Adventurers who had underwritten their move from Europe to America. They enjoyed trade with the native population until driven out by the French in 1632. The French gained control and built Fort Pentagoet to preserve their claim to the area. It is thought the fort was likely built on the Pilgrims' trading-post land. The British drove out the French in 1654. For the next 40 years, the French and British fought for control of Fort Pentagoet. Around 1665, the Baron de Castin arrived on the scene and married Chief Madockawando's daughter Mathilde. The town is named after him. The Dutch briefly captured Castine in 1674.

The peninsula, at the confluence of the Bagaduce River and the Penobscot Bay, was considered a prime location for defense of the inland and as a trading center. Therefore, the struggle for control continued, but after a while Fort Pentagoet was abandoned. In 1760, colonists of English descent resettled the site at the fort. The first permanent settlement, Penobscot, was established in 1761. Meanwhile, the British were driving out the French settlers in Acadia. The Acadians in exile, the 'cajuns, settled in parishes along the Mississippi River around New Orleans. In 1765, Acadian refugees were transferred from detention camps at Halifax, now under British control, to what became St. Martin County and Parish.

Throughout the American Revolution, the boundaries between American, British, French, and Dutch colonies remained in dispute. During the Revolution, the British built Fort George and dozens of smaller fortifications to establish their control of the region. In 1779, hundreds of British troops arrived from Halifax intending to create a haven for British loyalists in Castine. In July and August, the Revolutionary War battle called "The Penobscot Expedition" was the greatest United States naval failure until the attack on Pearl Harbor. When rebels retreated, they ran their ships aground, and set them on fire. America lost about 500 men and 43 ships due to their inability to engage in a complex, amphibious assault targeting Fort George. The losses have been attributed to mistrust and a lack of communication between ground and naval commanders and a lack of sufficient training for combatants. Castine was the last British post to be surrendered at the end of the American Revolution.

The news that the 1783 Treaty of Paris gave Castine to the United States was an unwelcome surprise to the Tory settlers who, in mass, dismantled their homes and shipped them north to found the town of St. Andrews on Passamoquoddy Bay. Castine, which was a part of Penobscot, was designated a custom house to collect revenue for the government on July 31, 1789. Castine remained part of Penobscot until 1796, when Penobscot and Castine were designated as two separate towns. After occupation of the town by the British during the War of 1812, Castine was made a port of entry to the United States. By 1825, the small rural town had 13 college graduates plus sea captains, whose education came from observation and travel. A graded school system was adopted in 1840 and a high school in 1850.

Castine today is the home of the Maine Maritime Academy, and the town is quite active, especially during the tourist and vacation season. The Castine Historical Society, Castine Scientific Society (Wilson Museum) and the Penobscot Historical Society are dedicated to preserving the history of the area. Along the streets are a number of signs explaining historical events and through this narrative walking tour, one can enjoy the lovely gardens and exquisite architecture, from Colonial days to the present. On a foggy day, the crunch of gravel underfoot, the dripping of the fog through the trees and the soft sounds of the harbor bell buoy contrast with the bellowing of the foghorns. The air has a clean, salty smell. There are soaring eagles and ospreys, seabirds, local and migrating birds, and seals foraging the river.

This story is about Solon J. Hanson, a sailor and fisherman, who lived here about 150 years ago when Castine was the epicenter of all merchant marine activities north of Boston. Solon's autobiography is told through his letters home from sea. Though technology has changed the fishing and shipping industries, the challenges and risks faced by seamen and their love of the sea remain defined by the persistent force of nature. Solon's adventures are action packed and his own words explain them best. Contextual annotation is woven around these letters to convey the perseverance, the love, the bravery and the hardships faced by the seamen and their families who defined American commerce in the pre-Civil War years.

CAULKERS.

Chapter 1

SOLON'S FATHER, CAPTAIN JOHN HANSON

OUR STORY BEGINS in Colonial America, when Maine was still part of the Massachusetts colony. In 1789, Castine launched its first recorded vessel, the 115-ton schooner *Ranger*, from the yard of Joseph and John Perkins at the foot of Dyer Lane. The ships *Orno* and the *John and Phoebe* were built in 1796, the same year Castine separated from the governance of Penobscot and incorporated as Castine. Support industries for the sailing industry sprung around the active shipyard. The increase in work attracted many people to the area.

Robert Hanson, born in 1784 in New Hampshire, the 13th child of John Hanson and Deliverence Clark, moved to Waldoboro, Massachusetts (now Maine) and then to Hancock County to work in the shipyards as a ship caulker. Robert was Solon J. Hanson's grandfather. Although family records do not show where and when he worked in the Castine shipyards, Robert likely worked on the 94-foot *Ruthy* in 1803 and the *Thucydides* in 1808.

The tools of a ship caulker were simple: oakum, mallets, and tar. The caulker was usually an independent worker, but bore the responsibility of ensuring that the ship would not leak during its voyage. Oakum, a loose fiber obtained by untwisting and picking hemp ropes, was used to fill crevices between boards. Caulkers used irons and longheaded mallets to force oakum into the seams, and then poured melted pitch or tar over the seam as a sealant. They and the other skilled craftsmen were employed as needed by the shipyards, usually for the duration of a contract to build a vessel. Sailors who specialized in caulking and other ship repair were employed for voyages since continual caulking was required en route on large sailing vessels.

The early 1800s was a time of conflict arising from international tensions and partisan politics between the federal powers of Jefferson's Republican Party, who supported the common farmers, and the Massachusetts powers dominated by the Federalist Party, who supported commercial interests like seaboard merchants. Castine was a stage where this conflict was dramatically acted out in military combat. The locals found themselves in both agricultural and merchant marine professions, and occasionally in combat.

On November 28, 1809, Robert married Sarah Hutchins. Sarah gave birth to John Hanson, Solon's father, March 31, 1811, in Castine. Robert and Sarah operated a family farm while Robert took various jobs in the shipyards and work in commerce. During warm months, corn, squash, potatoes, and onions were grown in gardens created in the rocky soil or atop the soil when rich riverbed sediments were hauled and laid like a blanket. Robert and his sons fished, sailed, and worked in shipyards. Sarah augmented the family income by selling surplus produce, sewing, tutoring, teaching, and taking on tenants. In the fall, after the farm harvest, men from Castine and Penobscot, including boys from the age of ten, went on community-funded fishing voyages for cod.

John's early years were influenced by military campaigns and the sights and sounds of a country at war in one of the busiest and oldest trade ports in the United States. The United States built Fort Madison, sometimes called Fort Porter, where Lt. A. Lewis commanded an artillery detachment armed with four 24-pound guns. Upon approach of British troops, Lewis blew up the magazine and retreated to Portland. Castine was occupied by the British during the War of 1812, when they ousted American troops from Fort George and Fort Porter (renamed it Fort Castine), and dug a canal across the peninsula's narrow neck, creating an island that was easier to defend. During the height of the occupation, some 4000 British troops were living in Castine. The British left on April 14, 1815; Castine was the last region in the United States to be occupied by British troops. Fort Castine was renamed Fort Madison in the Civil War.

The 1820, the year Maine separated from Massachusetts, the Penobscot census recorded Robert Hanson, a wife in the same age bracket, and a male under the age of ten, as being the only occupants in the household of a family farm. John Hanson was a studious, industrious, and devoutly religious individual. He attended grammar school in Penobscot. Even during his early years his ambition was to be a sea captain. After his grammar schooling, which included navigation, astronomy, geography, and comprehensive academic skills, his education would have included loose apprenticeships and tutoring in private homes.

Through his father's contacts at the shipyards, young John became interested in commerce and shipping work. He watched the building of the 111-foot *Canova*, which was launched in 1823 (one of her guns rests in the Castine Town Hall), the 115-foot *Antioch*, launched in 1826, and the 102-foot *Lucas*, launched in 1828.

John also took a great interest in Lucy Newberry Wardwell. Lucy and her brother Amos were the only children of Ebenezer (Eben) and Elizabeth Wardwell. Lucy's grandfather, Jeremiah Wardwell, was one of the founding fathers of the Penobscot merchant marine community and a man of influence. Jeremiah assisted in the original survey while working with John Peters. He served as captain of the First Company, Second Regiment, Second Brigade in the American Revolution. According to family stories, he taught young men math, surveying, and navigation before schools were established in the region. He was a selectman, one of the committee chosen to draw up the agreement of the separation of Castine and Penobscot, and a member of the committee chosen to divide the town into eight school districts and apportion students and funding to each district. In 1801, he and Captain Thatcher Avery provided funds to build Penobscot's first church building, a Methodist church on the farm of Captain Dunbar. In 1809, he built Penobscot's first schoolhouse.

Lucy Newberry Wardwell had a wonderful sense of humor and relayed the town's gossip in poignant New England style. Lucy, being from a highly respected family, was well educated and quite knowledgeable about sailing. John Hanson married Lucy Newberry Wardwell on November 13, 1832. Eight months later, their daughter Lucy Jane Hanson was born in Penobscot, on "July 14, 1833, Saturday night at 9 o'clock," according to the family Bible. The three resided on their family farm in North Castine.

It was not uncommon for wives of sea captains to accompany their husbands on voyages, as documented in Joan Druett's book *Hen Frigates*. When John became a sea captain, Lucy Newberry wrote to him of her longing to join him at sea. In his February 20, 1837, letter, the employment he mentions that Lucy Newberry has undertaken was midwifery, as her mother had done. There are no family records of her traveling at sea.

Family stories relate that John Hanson was eager to climb the ropes from ordinary sailor to mate to sea captain. Most of his work was on small trading voyages, or "coastals," along the eastern seaboard. Letters from John Hanson to his wife document that in 1834 he sailed for Captain Gray on a voyage from Castine to St. Lago De Cuba, to Trinidad, then to Boston and home. With Captain Gray, the sailors had prayers twice a week and formed a Temperance Society. Shipboard conditions sounded pleasant when compared to typical accounts of sailing in that era. In another letter, John documents his 1837 voyage to St. Joseph, Florida. Exactly when John Hanson became a sea captain is not known. Records show that Captain John Hanson was the master of the schooner *Conanchet* in 1840. The Penobscot 1840 census lists Robert and Sarah Hanson, Solon's grandparents, as the sole occupants of their farm. Then in their 50s, the couple worked mainly in agriculture. Robert became the vice president of the local Temperance Society.

Solon J. Hanson, "Sody," was born on August 10, 1838, in Penobscot, Maine. Surrounded by a community that was completely invested in merchant marine, it is little wonder that Solon's first and only wish was to become a sea captain like his father. The story of his career as a sailor and fisherman is told through his diary and his letters home from sea.

Solon's younger brother Amos Hanson, "Amy" or "Ame," arrived on October 2, 1840, "at 2 in the morning," according to the family Bible. With three young children and with older parents, Lucy Newberry felt the stress of maintaining a household and family farm while John was at sea. The Hanson family relocated to a house near the town commons in Castine. Presumably, they moved there so that during John's frequent and long-term absences, Lucy could find community support, and the children would be able to attend the local schools and Methodist Sunday School, both around the corner. An updated letter from John to his daughter Lucy Jane mentions the upcoming move, and thus it was probably written in 1843 or 1844.

Captain Hanson was the most influential person in Solon's life. The connection he had with his children despite his absence in person is evident in his letter to Lucy Jane:

> Well Lucy Jane I must give you a few words of advice . . .
> to begin You must never talk about your neighbors. Oh
> Lucy Jane it is the most Shocking thing in the world.

Never tattle I mean to tell stories from one to another it is very foolish indeed. Never condemn others for what you would do yourself. Finally, do to every one as you would wish to have them do to you, for the meet you measure to others shall be measured back to you again.

The significance of his letters today is that they capture that long-distance parental relationship. We hear so frequently about how parent-child relationships have changed throughout the years. Whether writing about the importance of reading every day or about when playtime should end, John's letters show that parenting six generations ago has much in common with parenting today.

THIS LETTER, DATED JULY 11, 1834, WAS WRITTEN BY JOHN HANSON IN ST. LAGO DE CUBA TO HIS WIFE LUCY NEWBERRY HANSON IN NORTH CASTINE.

St. Lago De Cuba July 11, 1834

We arrived here the 7th of July after a passage of 30 days and a very pleasant passage too for we have not had a storm or a gail of wind since we left home, which is something remarkable I have had very good health since I left home and every thing has you on with as much harmony as I could wish to have it.

Capt. Gray is quite an altered man. There is no mistake We have prayers twice a week. And have formed a Temperance Society on board and all joined it except one. It is rather unhealthy here at present we have cleansed our Brig and whitewashed every place that was nefressery. We can do no more but ask Heaven to protect us Times here are very dull sails cannot scarely be found for our lumber, and a cargo cannot be procured. We shall be discahrged in about a week and shall sail from here to Trinidad for a cargo. Which will detaine is about a fortnight.

Lucy _____ I shall write to you from Trinadad if there is a chance to get it conveyed to the States but if you should not receive one from there I want you to write me in Boston. Write your letter about the 20th of August direct to me Boston and git some one to carry it to Mr. Bryant and ask him to be so kind as to send it to Mr. Jehison. I shall certainly expect a leter from you it will be a __great consolation to me to hear from you, and that little childe

Give my fondest resspects to my Mother to all my Parents and Grandparents. Also to all enquireing friends.

*Lucy all my anxiety my prayers my wishes is for your health. be careful
of your self you know you have to be Husband wife Mother and all. Think
of this and them think you have a friend a companion that holds you dearer
than all – them – all – all*

Lucy kiss the babe for me.
And my prayers for you bouth is
that Heavan may grant you bouth
Health and strength
Pease and Plenty
always
yours
forever
John Hanson

**THIS LETTER DATED FEBRUARY 20, 1837, WAS WRITTEN BY JOHN HANSON
IN ST. JOSEPH, FLORIDA, TO HIS WIFE LUCY NEWBERRY HANSON IN NORTH
CASTINE, MAINE.**

Sent to Mrs J. Hanson North Castine M ___e
Florida   St Josephs   Feb 20th 1837

*Ever worthy and Affectionate Companion I arived here the 8th after a
passage of 26 days the worst I ever saw. I received your interesting as well a
amusing Letter the 14th with a heart everflowing with graditude to God for
his Mercy and goodness and to you for your attention and kindness.*

*I should have written before but thinking there was no time last and
wishing to know about when we shall be ready to Sail. I have water fill this
evening. tomorrow the mail leaves which takes this to you*

*The Last letter you wrote me I did not get but shall as soon as I get back
to N. York which will be about the 25 of next month As soon as you get this
letter have the goodness to write another and get it to N York by the time I
get there I shall come home from there at all events. Lucy the gift you ask is
in the care of the Creator and sustainer of mankind and through His goodness I hope it may be restored better and more worthy than when we last
parted. The Compliment deserves a present I shall not forget it.*

*I am glad to hear mother is so well. give my love to her. The part of your
letter you term "Striking" struck me with : He looked just like a mile in
length and she like a metate stone.*

Lucy I am much pleased with your employment I hope in about two months to see it The amount of money due Esq. Williams cannot be more than 12 or 14 dollars at most I am definely at a loss how to Account for the mistake but sure there is one. I suppose you had better let it stand untill I get home

Tell Lucy Jane I will get her a Bonnet to be a good girl and leav off crying.

Lucy if you have time and can as well as not you may make me a hat.

Lucy when you write again tell me about Fubathg and Mr Morrell an so . . .

Lucy I heard so much tell of St Josephs in N York I thought I should be almost tempted to moov here but I find it quite the contrary. were I doomd to stop here six months I should certainly die. I almost despise it. I think I shall give it up and take you to Texas. think of it and tell me how you should like to go there. But I suppose it will pussle you to tell being unaquainted with the history of the Country. I have got the history lately published, You shall see it when I come home

Lucy write me where the Coral will be when I get home . . .
Lucy I must now bid you good night.

> *wishing you more happiness than I could think of in a thousand years*
> *and all kind Heaven can bestow*
> *So prays your Constant Companion J Hanson*
> *To his wife L N Hanson*

STRAW BONNET.

THIS LETTER, UNDATED (AROUND 1843 OR 1844) FROM JOHN HANSON IN
BOSTON WAS WRITTEN TO HIS DAUGHTER LUCY JANE HANSON (ABOUT AGE
9) IN NORTH CASTINE.

Addressed to Miss Lucy J Hanson   Nth Castine Maine

Boston

My Dear Child

*I am very much pleased with the kind letter I received from you by the hand
of Mr Baher.*

*I am indead very Happy to know you are of that age and so far ad-
vanced in education as to be able to hold a corrispondence with me. You ask
me to excuse your bad writing why Lucy Jane there is not half the people in
the town can write as good a letter*

I am very much pleased with it indead

*You must write me every opportunity you have and write me a great
Long Letter and Strive to improve all that lays in your power You must
remember that all the names of Persons, places, rivers, mountains, xc. must
begin with a Capitil letter & the pronoun I. but the article a nead not be.*

*Well Lucy Jane I mus give you a few words of advice and then tell you
what I send you home*

*to begin you must never talk about your neighbours. Oh Lucy Jane it is
the most shocking thing in the world. never tattle I mean to tell stories from
one to another it is verry foolish very indead never Condem others for what
you would do yourself.*

*Finally do to every one as you would wish to have them do to you. for
the meet you measure to outhors shall be measured back to you again*

*When you moove to the Vilage My Dear Child you must not be in a
hurry to make aquandance. always think twice before you speak.*

*And further Lucy Jane I want you if you have the least regard for me
to pay the strictest attention to every command desire or wish of your Dear
Mother remember you can never half pay her for her care and attention
to you think how she has watched over you from your infancy untill now
with unremitting care and with what anxious hopes she has watched your
recovery in sickness, night and day Oh Lucy Jane how much you must love
her surely you could not disabey her. I now you couldn't.*

Well Lucy Jane I will now tell you what I am going to send you home.

*I have bought you a very pretty book and wrote your name in it and also
a testament a little pretty one and I have also Bought the same for Solon a*

pretty story book and testament and a picture book for Amy—I have wrote all your names in them Yes and when you get them you must not forget your poor Father. that has to work so hard and go through so much to make you comfortable and happy and be good Children and mind your Mother and learn all you can for that will pay me for all my cares and toils.

My Dear Child you must write to me again when I return from my next voyage and see what a good letter you will write

you must write me how my Solon and Amy gets along and if they are good boys. and if they are I will make you and them a pretty present and come home to see you I have sent home also a Box of shells to Mother and in it there is a lot in a paper for you I sent some of them and Like sent the rest. they are very good ones some of them are very pretty.

I did not send any to Solon or amy Because little boys do not want such things

I did not read your Books but I expect they are very good and suitable just such ones as you want.

I want you and Solon to read a chapter or more in your testaments every day and see how far you will get through it when I get home.

You must try to learn little Amy his litters this summer see if you can't before I get home if you will I will bring you something very pritty when I come for you and Amy bouth

Well Lucy Jane I don't think of anything else. at present to day is sunday I shall not send this untill tomorrow and if I think of anything I will write you a few lines tomorrow.

> *God bless you and give you a desire to do right*
> *So prays your Father*
> *John Hanson*

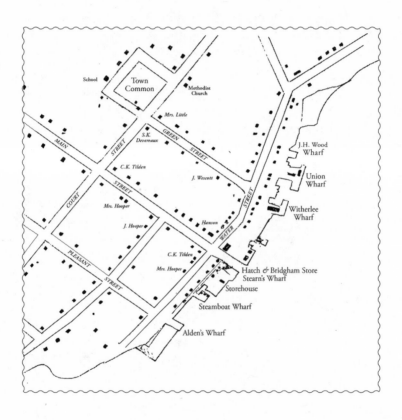

Chapter 2

THE NEW HOUSE IN CASTINE

AROUND 1843, THE FAMILY of Captain John Hanson moved to the heart of Castine, a community equally invested in the merchant marine. Lucy Newberry soon found support from her neighbors. The house near the town commons made it convenient for the children to attend grammar and Sunday school at the Methodist Church.

Lucy Newberry described Solon with pride:

> The children are all well, and they behave better than
> I expected . . . Solon goes to school all the time and
> learns very well, he never runs away, and never gets into
> trouble. He and Lucy J go to the Methodist Sunday
> School.

John's last letter to his daughter admonished her not to speak of scandal, however her mother, Lucy Newberry, penned some rather caustic gossip in her letter dated June 11, 1844. Time may soften our attitude toward the nature of her seemingly unflattering commentary. She undoubtedly spoke of friendly interactions with town folk to let John know that she had support from the community during her absence:

> I find Mr. Tilden a very kind neighbor. He has done
> everything but the thing itself, and with a little coaxing,
> I don't know but he would do that. He takes as much
> interest in the children, as he does his own. If he is as
> good as he seems to be he is a very good man.

Sometime at the end of 1844, Solon's Aunt Jane and her baby came to stay with the Hanson family for several years. According to family stories, when Lucy Newberry's mother, Elizabeth, died, Joanna Robbins, reportedly Lucy's cousin, came as housekeeper for Eben. Eventually, Eben married Joanna and they had a daughter, Jane Littlefield Wardwell. The letters do not indicate who Jane is; however, she is most likely Lucy Newberry's half sister. In the June 11, 1844, letter from Lucy Newberry to her husband John in Boston:

> Jane has left the class because Mrs. Town and the shop girls thought proper to do so. She writes to me that all the religion that she and all the Methodist churches has got put together is not sufficient to save the soul of a shit-poke. I suppose that would be termed a Franklin speech. She is coming home in about four weeks for good.

From later references to Aunt Jane's baby, it appears that Aunt Jane may be an unmarried mother-to-be. Perhaps this is the reason she is being ostracized from her schooling. Social values at this time frowned on pregnancy out of wedlock. Still, her local community would have accepted her. The Penobscot community followed religious beliefs that promoted acceptance instead of banishing those who didn't fit a mold. The gossip might be about a person's ostentatious display of wealth, flirtation, bragging, or drunkenness, but a line was drawn to maintain the dignity of all community members. Jane probably was not the victim of gossip or excessive scrutiny. Some years later, Jane Wardwell married Reverend Eben Hodgden, moved to Minneapolis and had a large family. Family stories do not record whether or not Reverend Hodgden was a Methodist.

In his letters to his children, John Hanson conveys his high esteem for education and religion. Lucy Jane and Solon were encouraged to read daily. Castine offered many academic opportunities. The family enthusiasm for learning was documented in subsequent letters and papers. Solon completed school in the Castine and Penobscot districts where education in the merchant marine was emphasized, and he became a sailor and fisherman. Amos, who was three years old, "keeps himself in candy by singing 'Old Nantucker' to the loafers" attended singing school locally and became an accomplished musician, poet, and sea captain. Amos wrote sea shanties like "Schooner Fred Dunbar," which was recorded by Gordon Bok in 1992 on his CD *Schooners*.

THIS LETTER DATED MARCH 30, 1844 WAS WRITTEN BY JOHN HANSON IN BOSTON TO HIS DAUGHTER LUCY JANE HANSON (AGE 10 YEARS OLD) IN CASTINE.

Letter addressed to Miss Lucy J Hanson   N Castine Maine

Boston March 30th 1844

My Dear Child

I got your letter enclosed in you Mothers to day for which you have my sincere thanks. I have wrote you once before by Mr Guy and you no doubt received [illegible] *before this My Dear Child* [several lines are illegible here] *say George H to take it a part* [illegible] *repaired it would be best for if you send it to Belfast* [illegible] *will always be playing on it and perhaps spout before you get it. but your Mother will know best. let her do as she pleases*

*   you have got your books before now I expect strive to make every improvement you can and help Sody to learn all you can.*

*   See if you can't get some chapters out of your little testaments to say to Mother out of the Book you and Sody too*

*   Kiss Sody and Amy for me and tell them to be good boys and mind Mother.*

*   God Bless you all. My Dear Babies*

*   So constantly prays you Father*
*   Good bye John Hanson*
*   To his Daughter L J Hanson*

The Dyce's Head Lighthouse was built in 1828 with a 42-foot tower on Jacob Dyce's farmland. The lantern windows are 130 feet above sea level and could be seen for 17 nautical miles.

**THIS LETTER DATED JUNE 11, 1844 FROM LUCY JANE HANSON IS VIRTUALLY
A GOSSIP RAG TO HER HUSBAND JOHN HANSON IN BOSTON.**

June 11, 1844

My Dear Husband

*I have received two letters from Caracoa, for which you have my warmest
thanks, I have been very uneasy about your health since you left Boston, but
you say you are better, God be praised, I am truly thankful I know I am, my
health is very good the children are all well, and they behave better than I
expected, I see it is not fashionable for children to behave, here, Solon goes to
school all the time and learns very well he never runs away, and never gets
into trouble he and Lucy J goes to the Methodist Sunday School, the Town
school will not begin before a month or two so Lucy J will have a long recess,
she has not been to school since last winter, Amos keeps himself in candy by
singing Old Nantucker to the loafers, he comes home very often with two
sticks of candy, and a pocket full of nuts, he is pretty noisey but he never
runs away so I call him a good boy, I feel very well contented here the house
is very good and very convient, but the company Oh Lord, from all parts of
the world every day some is acquinted with your Mother or Father, or mine,
and some has seen old Jonthum Stover, and he used to own part of the vessel,
and thousands comes because my Husband is a nice man, and that she devil
of Mrs Gools will help save my soul, for she will be my purgatory here upon
earth, and old Mrs Teb, lives in the back yard, and that is what I call para-
dise below, Mrs Atherton has called, she appears very friendly, she thinks
your health would be better if you should go to St. Peters, how do you like
soft sodder, Geo A E, has got the Post office, Mrs emerson has gone to Boston,
Mr J Hooper has gone to St Peters with Capt Devereux, Isiah Avery's wife
is dead she that was Sally Hooper, Peter Leach has lost his wife, and got a
pair of new trouser, Mr Pel Wescott and one of his sons both died in one
week Stephen Littlefield's wife has had a pair of twins, they come a little too
soon to be his, but she was sanctified about the time she was married, Esq
Hutchings Massy has got a pair of twins, your Father is Vice President of the
Temperance Society he gets along nicely, David W has got home he has been
to Belfast and come all smiles, Jane has left the class because Mrs town and
the shop girls thought proper to do so, she writs to me that all the religion
that she and all the Methodist chruches has got put together is not sufficient
to save the soul of a shitpoke, I suppose that would be termed a Franklin*

speech, she is coming home in about four weeks for good, Joel Perkins has moved to the Village, I heard the widow Jane was married I wish you would inquire, I find Mr Tilden a very kind neighbor he has done everything but the thing itself and with a little coaseing I dont know but he would do that, he takes as much interest in the children, as as he does his own, if he is as good as he seems to be he is a very good man, well my love when will you find yourself at home with your Lucy and the babies Oh Time speed on Oh how slow the time passes when we are looking for those we love, but when they are going to leave us how different oh if you could stop at home while the vessel went a voyage how happy i should be, but that would be too much happiness so I give it up as an impossibility. Oh John how I should like to go with you to some healthy place, I dont see why I cant I have been a very good Girl since you went away, I shall be glad when the children are larger so I can go a voyage with yo once or twice a year, just to keep your spirits up, you would not think time was Eternity if I was with you, do you think you would, Oh my dear Husband if I could only live near you I would not mind being Seasick all the time, but we must wait with patience time will bring forth all things

   Lucy Jane will write in a few days and then I will write a little in her letter.

   Oh John when you get to Boston fly home, I cant wait for you to come by steam, I must now bid you good bye wishing you every blessing kind heaven can bestow, may the Lord bless my dear John with health and happiness this shall be the constant prayer of your devoted Wife L N H to her own J H

     sent to Capt John Hanson   Boston Ms
        to the care of L W Hall
        postmarked Castine Me Jun 12   postage cost 18 3/4

ON THE ENVELOP, LUCY JANE HAS WRITTEN:

   I want A barrel of flour and half
   1 wooden bottomed horary
   I want them for my best kitchen

**IN HIS LETTER DATED JUNE 28, 1844, JOHN HANSON, TEMPORARILY IN
BOSTON, WRITES FATHERLY ADVICE TO HIS DAUGHTER LUCY JANE HANSON
(AGE 10 YEARS OLD) IN CASTINE.**

Boston June 28/44

My Dear Child

*I received your kind letter last week and am happy to learn you are so well
pleased with your new home.*

You must be a good girl and be careful and make good acquaentance.

*Dear Lucy Jane I wish you to consider you are old enough for people to
take notice of your conduct and you can't be to careful May God grant you
may always be worthy of the name of woman.*

Dear Child I am quite unwell but I hope to see you in a little while.

*I should be very glad to have you here you would be so much company
but you cannot come alone I have nothing new. May God Bless you your
Father*

John Hanson

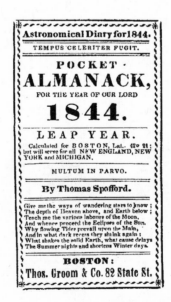

☾ *Last Quar.* Fri. 7th, 3. 46. e. N.
● New Moon, Sat. 15th, 7. 42. e. N. w
☽ *First Quar.* Sun. 23rd, 10. 38. m. E.
○ Full Moon, Sun. 30th, 1. 30. m. s.

M.W. Days.	☉ rises.	☉ sets.	☽ rises.	☽ south.	Full Sea.	☉'s decl.
1 S	4 33	7 27	8 35	0 16	11 35	22 7
2 *f*	4 32	7 28	9 27	1 20	morn.	22 15
3 M	4 32	7 28	10 10	2 20	0 27	22 22
4 T	4 31	7 29	10 46	3 17	1 14	22 29
5 W	4 31	7 29	11 17	4 9	2 2	22 36
6 T	4 30	7 30	11 43	4 57	2 50	22 42
7 F	4 30	7 30	morn.	5 42	3 39	22 48
8 S	4 29	7 31	0 10	6 26	4 31	22 53
9 *f*	4 29	7 31	0 35	7 9	5 30	22 59
10 M	4 28	7 32	1 0	7 52	6 34	23 3
11 T	4 28	7 32	1 29	8 36	7 33	23 7
12 W	4 28	7 32	2 0	9 21	8 35	23 11
13 T	4 28	7 32	2 34	10 7	9 31	23 15
14 F	4 27	7 33	3 14	10 55	10 14	23 18
15 S	4 27	7 33	4 1	11 45	10 55	23 20
16 *f*	4 27	7 33	sets.	ev. 34	11 33	23 23
17 M	4 27	7 33	8 50	1 23	ev. 7	23 24
18 T	4 27	7 33	9 24	2 11	0 42	23 26
19 W	4 27	7 33	9 56	2 59	1 17	23 27
20 T	4 27	7 33	10 25	3 46	1 53	23 27
21 F	4 27	7 33	10 52	4 32	2 33	23 28
22 S	4 27	7 33	11 18	5 17	3 17	23 27
23 *f*	4 27	7 33	11 46	6 5	4 5	23 27
24 M	4 27	7 33	morn.	6 57	4 59	23 25
25 T	4 27	7 33	0 20	7 52	6 7	23 24
26 W	4 27	7 33	0 58	8 49	7 11	23 22
27 T	4 27	7 33	1 41	9 51	8 23	23 20
28 F	4 27	7 33	2 35	10 54	9 29	23 17
29 S	4 28	7 32	3 38	11 57	10 24	23 14
30 *f*	4 28	7 32	4 49	morn.	11 21	23 10

June is in reality in our climate, what the poets represent May to be, the most lovely month in the year. Summer is commenced, and warm weather thoroughly established without oppressive heat. The trees and fields look proudly in the lustiness of their young green; and the sun shoots out his sultry strength, making the winged tribes wanton and noisy with their joy.

1	Very High Tides. *Fine*
f	TRINITY SUN. *weather*
3	Gt. Eartq. N. Eng. 1744.
4	☽ S. *for vegetation, if not*
5	Virgin's Spike south 8. 24.
6	Arcturus south 9h. 6m. e.
7	*too dry.* [Frost N.E. 1816.
8	Low Tides. ☽ J. Cold &
f	1st Sun. af. Trinity. ☽ H.
10	*Fine showers, vegetation*
11	*revives and comes forward*
12	☽ Apogee. *rapidly.*
13	☽ 7*s. *Hot and sultry.*
14	V's greatest brilliancy.
15	☉ eclipsed invisible.
f	High Tides. Great eclipse
17	☽ Ma- [of the sun 1806.
18	17th Bunker Hill Battle, 1775
19	☽ V. *Appearance of rain.*
20	Antares south 10h. 26m. e.
21	☉ en. C. Summer Sols.
22	M. gr. elon. *Hot and dry*
f	3rd S. af. T.☉qr. J. [Tides
24	St. John Baptist. [Low
25	*The clouds denote rain and*
26	*if the signs fail not vege-*
27	☉ H. *tation will now come*
28	☽ Perigee. *forward with*
29	St. Peter & St. Paul's day.
f	4th af. T. V. sta. *rapidity.*

Farmers' Calendar.—Now let every farmer be at home and attend to his business. The cattle will not then break into the mowing grounds and corn fields; the boys will be kept busy and the women will not scold for want of oven-wood. A stitch in time saves nine; which means, with other things, that it is better to drive the blue heifer out of the oats before the rest of the cattle find the breach in the fence.

The rolling Planets and the glorious sun,
Still keep that order which they first begun ;
But wretched *man* alone, has gone astray,
Swerv'd from his God, and walks another way

If you invite one to your house, show him a friendly behaviour and an open countenance ; it is a flagrant sin against the laws of hospitality to open your door and shut your benignity.

Eternal Maker, hail ! hail power divine !
The Heav'n and Earth, the day and night are thine ;
Matter and form to *Thee,* their being owe,
From Thee, their original, they flow,

To *spin* with art, in ancient times, has been
Tho't not beneath the noble dame or Queen :
From that employ, our maidens had the name
Of *Spinsters,* which they now disclaim ;
But since to *Cards* each female turns her mind,
And to that dear delight is so inclined,
Change the soft name of *Spinster* to a harder
And let each damsel now, be called a *Carder*

HUMAN LIFE.

Ah, what is life ! a dream within a dream !
A pilgrimage, from peril rarely free !
A barque that sails upon a changing sea,
Now sunshine and now storm ; a mountain stream,
Heard, but scarce seen, ere to the dark deep gone ;
A wild star blazing with unsteady beam,
Yet for a season fair to look upon,
Like as an infant on Affection's knee.
A youth now full of hope and transient glee ;
In manhood a peerless noon now bright, anon,
A time-worn ruin, silvered o'er with years.
Life is a race where slippery steps arise,
Where discontent and sorrow are the prize,
And when the goal is won, the grave appears.

TIDES.—Time to be added to the Moon's southing to find the time of High Water at the following places ; also the rise of the water in feet.

Albany . .	3 30	1	Montaug p. .	7 33	6
Amboy . .	8 15	5	Mount Desert	11 2	13
Annapolis .	11 12	3	Nantucket .	12 0	11
Baltimore .	1 36	3	Narrows, N.Y.	8 2	6
Bay Fundy .	12 10	60	N Bedford .	7 39	6
Block Island	7 38	5	Newburyport	11 15	5
BOSTON . .	11 30	11	New Haven .	10 17	10
Cape Ann .	11 30	11	New London .	8 56	8
Cape Cod .	11 30	6	Newport . .	7 51	3
Cape Fear .	8 1	5	NEW YORK	8 56	6
Cape Hatteras	9 1	5	Norwalk . .	10 54	3
Cape Henlopen	8 45	5	Norwich . .	10 56	3
Cape Henry .	7 51	6	Philadelphia .	2 5	1
Cape Look't.	9 4	5	Plymouth . .	11 30	6
Cape May .	8 45	5	Portland . .	10 45	13
Castine . .	11 0	12	Portsmouth .	11 15	10
Charleston. .	7 15	5	Providence .	8 25	5
Eastport . .	11 30	25	Quebec, Can. .	8 12	3
Fairfield . .	10 58	6	Riverhead . .	9 52	6
Halifax. N. S.	7 30	9	Sag Harbour .	10 0	5
Hartford . .	9 25	1	Salem . . .	6 37	5
Hell Gate .	9 35	6	Sandy Hook .	11 30	5
Ipswich . .	11 15	10	Savannah . .	12 0	0
Lubeck . .	11 30	25	Saybrook . .	11 43	6
Machias . .	11 30	16	Southold . .	9 52	5
Marblehead .	11 30	11	Whitestone .	11 30	3
Marth. V. .	7 37	7	York, Me. . .	10 47	13

ALMANACKS AND REGISTERS.—The subscriber, [author of this Almanack, and also of the astronomical part of several of the most popular Annual Registers and Almanacks in the United States and the British provinces,] respectfully informs the public that he is prepared to furnish the Calculations for Almanacks and Registers for any place, and for any year. Having made them for this place for fifty years in advance, he is able to alter them to suit for any other, at far shorter notice and less expense than any astronomer who has to calculate originally for a particular place.
New York, Aug. 1843. THOS. SPOFFORD.

*A "dog-type" of Solon Hanson and Captain John Hanson.
Perhaps this is the book he mentions sending from Boston.*

Chapter 3

LEARN ME NAVIGATION

I N CASTINE AND PENOBSCOT, love and knowledge of boating is and
was paramount. In the 1800s, most of the region's businesses were
in some way related to the merchant marine industry. In addition
to having shipyards and the homes of many sailors, sea captains, and
merchant marine investors, Castine had a number of support businesses
including rope walks, tin shops, blacksmiths, pump and block makers,
coopers and bakers.

Skilled workmen in the trades of rigging, caulking, painting, carpen-
try, joining, and sail making, not only built vessels, but also could do
repairs on incoming vessels. They constructed large vessels such as the
William Jarvis, launched in 1848. Likewise, regional public and private
education focused on aspects of the merchant marine and sailing. Such
an environment instilled in young men the ambition of a career at sea.

A series of six letters from Lucy Jane and Solon document a voyage
Captain Hanson made in 1846. A common thread in these letters is the
family's anxiety over knowing Captain Hanson's itinerary. Understanding
the remarkable role of the 1800s sea captain leads to a better understanding of this apprehension. The captain of the ship was familiar with all
aspects of ship operation and could fill any of the roles of his crew. Captains required expert skills in navigation, and had the sole responsibility
for navigating their ships. As an entrepreneur, the captain of a trading
vessel was businessman, independent contractor, marketer, and work-for-
hire man.

The captain was ultimately responsible for the lives of the crew and
passengers; the condition of the ship; and the loading, safekeeping, trans-

port, and delivery of the cargo. Sailing independent ships rather than packet ships meant finding enough customers to make a profitable voyage. At each port, he had to find someone wanting to hire a crew to ship some cargo. At port, the captain was responsible for arranging for repairs, inspection, customs, pilotage, and towing. The captain also acquired fresh provisions for the crew and saw to their medical needs. If a sailor left his position, the captain would have to find a replacement. Being a sea captain was a job learned partially through advanced education but mostly through apprenticeship and years of experience. In recompense, the captain enjoyed the privacy of his own cabin on the starboard side. The captain wasn't always able to secure business at his intended destination. Thus, Captain Hanson was probably not able to give his family a complete itinerary when he departed on this trading voyage.

There are no further family records that would indicate the business Captain Hanson undertook in 1846 and 1847. However, Captain John Hanson is listed as master of the schooner *Eglantine* in 1847 in a book titled *The Leaches of Penobscot, Part VI, Sea Captains of Penobscot* (self-published by Mark E. Honey, 1997). The family letters of the era mention some of the stops he made: Kingston, Holmes Hole, a harbor on Martha's Vineyard, and Boston. Amid the references to his location, Solon and Lucy Jane express their interest in geography:

> Mother has boxed up your chart . . . Mother has wrote
> to you to buy me a dress I don't know which I had a
> dress or geography and an atlas . . . if you get me a ge-
> ography get me Olney's

Lucy Jane requested that her father buy her a copy of *Olney's Geography* when in Boston. Jessie Olney (1798–1872) wrote the *Practical System of Modern Geography*, published in 1828, and *A New and Improved School Atlas to Accompany the Practical System of Modern Geography*, published around 1831. These were standard grammar school texts at the time. Solon relayed in an undated letter, probably written in 1847, that he was studying Olney's Geography.

In spite of their concerns over Captain Hanson's whereabouts, Solon was a happy child by all accounts. Little is documented about how Solon spent his early days. After his schoolwork was completed, Solon fished from shore to bring home supper, provided care for his little brother Amos, and spent time in the shipyards learning from the craftsmen and sailors.

While dreaming of going to sea with his father, Solon spent free time playing and exploring the Castine peninsula. "My sled is getting kinder give out here," Solon wrote in one letter. In another letter, he mentioned his brother Amos and Dan Bridges (a neighbor) "digging back of the fort behind an old stump for babies." The "babies" he referred to might be mushrooms or bullets or cannonballs. Castine had three forts where exploration was possible. Fort Pentagoet was built around 1626 on the water's edge as an outpost settlement. Fort George was built by the British and saw battle during the American Revolution. Fort Madison was built in 1811 as defense during the War of 1812. Playing at the forts remains a pastime today.

Old photograph of Fort George

A LETTER DATED NOVEMBER 13, 1846, FROM SOLON (AGE 8) TO HIS FATHER, REVEALS THAT HE MISSES HIS FATHER.

Nov. 13, 1846

My Dear Father I want to See you very much its not quite a week and it Seems a year since you left home mother his getteng Supper She Said She was going to finish her letter this evening I wish I knew where you was a going this winter Sometimes I fear you will never get back again and I had rather bee with you fore what could a little boy like me without a father do I couldant do nothing a tall you don't know how we miss you evenings I want to See you So I am almost dead I wish you would write me a good long Letter when you arrive at Boston my School will be done in two weeks from now and I am very Sorry do father give me directions for the winter if I do as you tell me I know I shall do right Mother Says we Shall have a lonesome winter without any Papa and I think So to if I am a good boy

*and learn all I can will you let me go with you next Spring wont you father
I wish you could stay to home this winter Mother looks as Sober as if She
never wanted you to go to Sea again Lucy Jane has not come home yet Jane
and the baby here yet the little dear laught every time I Sing doodnords
doodnords as Same as you used to Sing then I ask him if he wants to See
his unker John and he looks up in my face as to Say yes Dear Father I have
nothing More to write I must now bid you good bye wishing you a pleasant
voyage and a speedy return home*

>*From your Dutifull Son*
>*Solon Hanson*

**LUCY JANE (AGE 13) WROTE THIS LETTER DATED NOVEMBER 24, 1846 TO
HER FATHER AT A BOSTON ADDRESS.**

Sunday Evening Nov the 24 1846
My Dear Father

*I am very happy to have the opportunity of writing to you this evening Amos
is making such a noise that I cant hardly write dear father I am very happy
to hear that you arrived in Kingston safely and I am sorry to hear that you
are sick Mother has boxed up your chart and so we put our letters in to save
the postage Aunt Jane says that she shall not put her's in the box because she
is afraid that you will not think to open the box not until you are at sea I
hope that you Like Convers give my love to Eben and Con tell Con. him to
be a good boy and not run about E'nights after he gets in boston you dont
know how Amos has learned he reades in the young reader Dear father
Mother has wrote to you to buy me a dress I dont know which I had rather
have a Dress or a geography and an Atlas I know that kneed the Dress most
I almost wish that I had both but I dont expect to have them so I shant say
a word about it Dear father I try to improve all I can and I hope to be very
much improved when you get back Aunt Jane is putting Ideas into Solons
head I cant think of much to write so I believe I must close*

>*Answer this in Boston*
>*Yours Sincerly Lucy J Hanson*
if you get me a geography get me Olney's
you must excuse
those little Fs
I was in a hurry

THIS LETTER FROM SOLON HANSON (AGE 8) TO HIS FATHER WAS PROBABLY
WRITTEN EITHER SUNDAY NOVEMBER 24, 1846 ALONG WITH HIS SISTER'S
OR SUNDAY DECEMBER 29, 1846.

Castine Sunday evening 29th 1846

My Dear father

*I am very happy to here that you have arrived at Kingston safely Amos and
Dan bridges have been diging back of the fort behind an old Stump for
babies but they couldant find any so they come home without one I feel very
glad to write you Lucy Jane has been biting off her finger nails to think of
Something to write to you and I cant think of anything of anything if I bite
ever So much*

*Dear Father I send My love to you and Eben and son and Mr Hatch
Oh Father I wish I was agoing with you this winter I thought I would write
a letter to you this evening because I dident have nothing to do and So I
thought I would write a letter to you when I get older or no more I will
write you a better letter as I am very much put to it for words I will bid you
good bye*

*From your dutiful Son
Solon Hanson*

THIS UNDATED LETTER WAS PROBABLY WRITTEN DECEMBER 6, 1846 FROM
SOLON HANSON (AGE 8) TO HIS FATHER IN BOSTON.

[Addressed to Capt. John Hanson Boston, Mass.]

Castine Sunday 6th 1846

My Dear Father

*My School is done and I have nothing to do and I wish I was with you
now, I suppose I shall have a lonesome winter without you for ive nothing
to do and cant Sleep all the time I cant Stay in the House all the time please
Father tell me how many hours to Stay in the street Father do you think it
is best for me to have boots this winter Mother Says it will not pay the last
letter that I wrote was very foolish and I thought this would be worse than
that Amos learns very fast his School is done to and I am agoing to learn
him as fast as I can I am agoing to learn to cypher in the evenings Mother*

*is sick and making a dreadful fuss Sarah is making herb tea I have nothing
more to write*

*So now I will bid you good bye wishing
you good health and a pleasant voyage
from your Dutiful Son
Solon Hanson*

Solon relished his schoolwork. He diligently studied arithmetic and geography along with his three classmates. During these years, home educated ladies like Abigail and Sarah Hawes taught in the area, as described

Binnacle

in *Abigail and Sarah Hawes of Castine: Navigators and Educators*, written by Mark E. Honey and published in 1996. Early education included reading, writing, science, and language at school, plus reinforcing these skills at home. Geometry, logic, and other skills of navigation were taught to older students. All of these skills were preparing him for a career at sea.

Throughout his correspondence, Solon writes like the typical eight-year-old wishing to spend time with his father. Captain Hanson could little ignore his request:

I hope you will get home time enough to learn me
Navigation.

When home, Captain Hanson did spend time teaching his sons the skills of navigation. He probably showed Solon a copy of *The New American Practical Navigator*, by Nathaniel Bowditch, published in 1801. Bowditch reduced the mathematics of navigation to a level attainable by every sailor that understood basic arithmetic. Bowditch further explained methods of finding latitude, wind conditions, and currents, and he defined plotting procedures, and personal responsibilities. The book became an essential navigator's tool on board most vessels.

Navigation is the art of plotting a course between two locations without the use of land reference. Closely related, piloting is the art of finding geographic location when land is in sight. The tools of navigation in use in the mid-19th century included log

Sextant

"chips," harpoon logs, compasses, lead lines, chronometers, sextants, and plotting tools such as parallel rulers, dividers, navigational tables, nautical almanacs, and charts. It was the first mate's responsibility to record relevant information, such as weather conditions, ship's speed, number of sails, and heading, in the ship's logbook.

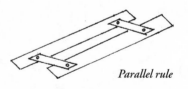

Protractor

A ship's speed was measured with the log "chip" beginning in the 1400s. The log chip consisted of a weighted, buoyant piece of wood attached to a rope, the "log line." The rope was knotted at fractional intervals of a nautical mile and had a special flag close to the weight and at a distance such that when observed over the stern, the weight was known to be beyond the ship's wake. The knots were 1/120th of a nautical mile. A nautical mile is approximately 6080 feet, whereas a statute mile is 5280 feet: by definition, 60 nautical miles equals one degree of latitude. The rope was spooled on a reel stored on the aft railing. A 30 second sand hourglass was kept with the reel.

Two sailors were needed to take a measurement of speed. The first would heave the weight over the stern while the second held the reel up high. When the second spotted the flag, the weight was beyond the ship's wake and could be considered a fixed position. The timer was started and the rope unreeled at a rate equal to the ship's speed. After 30 seconds, the line

Parallel rule

was held back so no additional rope would unreel. The length of the rope that unreeled in 30 seconds was divided by 30 to get the speed. The length could be estimated by the number of knots, each being 1/120th of a nautical mile. Multiplying by 120 half minutes per hour is the same as dividing by 30 seconds. This gave the rate of nautical miles per hour. Thus the number of knots let out was equal to the ship's nautical miles per hour or "knots."

The ship's direction, or heading, was determined by compass readings. Ship's compasses had special packaging to protect the compass needle and its movement from extreme weather conditions. Knowledge of compass usage and its idiosyncrasies was imperative for sailors. Roger

Duncan makes mention in his book, *Coastal Maine: A Maritime History*, of a ship at sea that was struck by lightening twice in one day. This caused the iron freight to become magnetized and then their compasses did not work until it demagnetized. Deviation errors, or errors arising from on-board metal that gave the magnet false readings, were remedied by special housing, which shielded or compensated for local magnetic fields. Variation errors are deviations from the magnetic north pole to the true North Pole. The deviation from true north was determined from charts or alma-nacs and a rough knowledge of the ship's latitude and longitude.

The ship's speed and direction provided necessary velocity informa-tion for "deduced reckoning" or "ded reckoning." The mate had to esti-mate deviations from the measured velocity due to winds, "leeward drift," and current. Since the course was plotted according to the heading and distance traversed, a compass reading was recorded with every change in heading. Deduced reckoning course lines were drawn as a connected path of straight lines on a chart. The first mate would position the parallel rulers so that one would pass through the compass rose in the direction of the true heading. The distance of the course was taken as the product of the ship's speed and the amount of time passed. He then found the map scaled distance by positioning a pair of dividers on the chart's mile scale. Using the dividers to transfer this distance to the line of the course, he drew the course line on the chart.

Errors in the velocity could lead to significant errors in the ship's de-duced position. This was especially true for long voyages between con-tinents. It could prove equally disastrous near shallows. The position could be refined with additional input. Soundings were measured with a lead weight, typically 7 to 14 pounds, attached to a rope about 10 to 20 fathoms long. The rope was marked in fathoms, each six feet. Measured depths were compared to depths annotated on charts to correct the posi-tion and to avoid shallow water.

It was the captain's responsibility to determine the ship's position in-dependently from the first mate's deduced reckoning and using different instruments. Latitude and longitude were measured at noontime with a sextant, a nautical almanac, and a chronometer. The altitude or angle from the horizon of the sun above the water was measured using a sextant. This angle depends on day, month, year, and latitude. Starting about 30 min-utes before the estimated local noon, sightings are taken for a period of an hour. The maximum height of the sun above the horizon is local noon. The latitude is then determined from a navigational table in the nautical almanac. Since the altitude angle of Polaris, the North Star, equals the latitude of the vessel, latitude could also be determined on a clear night.

Longitude was computed by subtracting the local time from the vessel's onboard chronometer reading Greenwich time. Local noon occurs when the sun is at its maximum altitude and hence is lying along the same meridian line as the vessel. For each hour difference, there is a 15° longitude difference from Greenwich meridian. This is because the earth rotates 360° in 24 hours, or in other words it turns 15° each hour.

According to *Longitude*, by Dava Sobel, accurate chronometers were first invented by John Harrison in 1762 and were perfected by the 1800s. Accuracy at sea requires that a clock neither gain nor lose more than three seconds per day, or else the errors introduced over the course of the voyage will yield errors in the accuracy of the longitude. Three seconds per day corresponds to about fifteen nautical miles over a three-week voyage. The saga of the quest for an accurate methodology for determining longitude at sea is a powerful part of maritime history. One proposed solution was to establish a gridded network of ships with the task of sounding cannon blasts at certain hours.

Together the captain and his first mate determined the ship's position and the new heading toward his destination. The captain used his tools to get a true "fix" or geographic latitude and longitude of the vessel at noontime. This fix validated the deduced reckoning of the first mate.

THIS UNDATED LETTER WAS PROBABLY FROM EARLY 1847 (IT REFERENCES THE NEW YEAR) FROM LUCY JANE (AGE 11) AND FROM SOLON HANSON (AGE 8) TO THEIR FATHER.

My Dear Father

Mother has written in her letter that i would speak for myself but what to say I do not know, I am never put to it for words except when I am writing to you. When Mother got your letter last eve I and Amy had gone over to see Maria, we had a very pleasant time indeed, but I had a more pleasant time when I returned and found a letter from you I hope that you will not go any farther than N P. don't you George Dyer says that they are going to put a tailors shop up down at the island next summer and the girls are hired to work by the piece, and I think some of going down dont you think it would be better than any other place? I do, because it is more retired the proprieter is a married man with two children and a cripple at that. I forgot to wish you a happy New Year I had a very happy one indeed and I hope yours was the same. I suppose that I shall have to leave the other side for Sode or the old Harry will be raised but I could not stop to write anymore very well for it is most one oclock So wishing you a prosperous voyage and a quick return home I remain your ever aff daughter

Lucy J Hanson

ON THE REVERSE OF LUCY JANE'S LETTER, SOLON WRITES TO HIS FATHER "I HOPE YOU WILL GET HOME TIME ENOUGH TO LEARN ME NAVIGATION."

My Dear father

we received your kind letter last night and thought you were as far as holmes hole at any rate but I am glad that you are as far as you were when you wrote everything is going on well at school I study grammer and Arithmatic we are going to have another exibition at the end of this term I shall belong to it.

As for this winter droging I dont believ but very little in it if i do dabbe I hope you will get home time enough to learn me Navigation.

my old sled is getting kinder give out here, thier and I have just benn Doctering her a little and sick Mother says that I had better exclaim with the Poet as Eaton did when he wrote to his wife

Come Hilanders Let us be a marching
Each one now his true love a Sarching

from your Dutiful Son
Solon Hanson
To his Father John Hanson

Excuse the writing

THIS LETTER FROM SOLON WAS PROBABLY WRITTEN EARLY IN 1847 WHEN HIS FATHER MADE IT BACK TO BOSTON.

My Dear Father

I am glad to hear that you have arrived safe at Boston I have been sick the first part of the winter but now I am well again and go to School and I study Olney's geography and grammer and Arithmatic their are but four grammer boys in School and I have the honor of being one of them Amos has improved Considerable And he is in the young Reader My Dear Father I hope that you will but come home I cant beare to think of your going away again you must come home and wait till the new vessail is done and then you must let me go with you I am going to be as good boy as I can and try to do everything that I CAn to try to please you and Mother I have nothing to write in particular for Amy is gone to Singing School and I promised to come after him at recess and so I bid you good bye
wishing you a pleasant passage

from your Dutiful Son
Solon Hanson

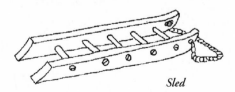

Sled

A schooner on the Bagaduce. Dyce's Head Lighthouse is on the coastline to the left and Castine Habor is on the right.

Chapter 4

SOLON AS COOK'S MATE

IN 1850, AT THE AGE of twelve, Solon's dream of joining his father at sea came true. On November 17, Solon wrote to his mother from Hallowell, a town close to Augusta, Maine, on the Kennebec River. The letter reflects his enthusiasm and courage. To his mother he expressed great pride in shooting a Cape Drake, nickname along the Maine coast for a red-throated loon, and in fixing dinner when the cook was incapacitated. As a youngster on board, his first-known assignment was as cook's assistant.

As a cook's mate, Solon was all too familiar with the standard sea fare. Castine had a business that made sea rations like "hardtack." The recipe for hardtack is similar to today's recipe for children's playdough. One pound of flour is mixed with one tablespoon of salt and enough water to form firm dough. Other recipes for hardtack have different ratios of flour, lard, and yeast. The dough is spread flat on a metal cooking sheet, divided and baked at 250°F for 2 to 3 hours. Served for a meal, the hardtack had to be soaked in coffee or some other liquid, because it was as hard as New England granite. Hardtack often became infested with worms or insects.

Solon mentions making "Bread for Dinner." This was another term for "Cracker Hash." To make "Cracker Hash," the hardtack was pounded to a powder (back to flour, basically) and water and jam or some other sweetener like molasses was added. The mixture stirred and baked in a pan on the stove in the galley.

Solon probably made a family favorite, "Slumgudgen." This is a dish consisting of scrambled eggs with torn bits of bread and small pieces of salt pork or salted meat. Edwin Solon Conner, the grandson of Lucy Jane

Hanson, used to prepare slumgudgen when he was a cook on fishing expeditions to the Grand Banks. Edwin told his grandchildren that when the galley ran out of chicken eggs, he would row ashore and would gather gull eggs for a not too tasty, but equally hearty fare.

The list on the back of Solon's letter provides a possible clue to the voyage father and son were taking. Given the itinerary they allude to, and the fact they kept apace with a schooner, they were on a coaster, hauling freight between ports along the eastern seaboard. This type of trade is akin to that of modern-day air carriers and truckers. Ships hauled cargo from one port to the next providing an economical means to exchange produce, raw materials, and manufactured products. A number of records exist that establish the basic values of traded items. Goods exchanged were sometimes recorded in quantities of quintals, bushels, and barrels.

Solon's generation was inspired by Richard Dana's book, *Two Years Before the Mast* (1832). Many books that compile historic information about sailing reference Dana's book. The following passage illustrates the feelings of a young sailor on the sailing vessel:

> One night, while we were in these tropics, I went out to the end of the flying-jib-boom, upon some duty and, having finished it, turned round and lay over the boom for half an hour, admiring the beauty of the sight before me. Being so far out from the deck, I could look at the ship as a separate vessel;—and there, rose up from the water, supported only by the small black hull, a pyramid of canvass, spreading out far beyond the hull and towering up almost, as it seemed in the indistinct night air, to the clouds. The sea was as still as an inland lake; the light trade-wind was gently and steadily breathing from astern; the dark blue sky was studded with tropical stars; there was not a sound but the rippling of the water under the stern; and the sails were spread out on each side, twenty or thirty feet beyond the deck; the top-most studding sails, like wings to the top-sails; the top-gallant studding sails spreading fearlessly out above them, still higher, the two royal studding sails, looking

like two kites flying from the same string; and, highest of all, the little sky-sail, the apex of the pyramid, seemed actually to touch the stars, and to be out of reach of human hand. So quiet, too, was the sea, and so steady the breeze, that if these sails had been sculptured marble they could not have been more motionless. Not a ripple upon the surface of the canvass; not even a quivering of the extreme edges of the sail—so perfectly were they distended by the breeze. I was lost in the sight, that I forgot the presence of the man who came out with me, until he said (for he, too, rough old man-of-war's-man as he was, had been gazing at the show) half to himself, still looking at the marble sails—"How quietly they do their work!"

The ship Richard Dana is describing is a tall ship, basically a large square-rigged vessel with three or more masts. The expression "before the mast" refers to the fact that sailors were housed in the forecastle, the superstructure at the bow of the merchant ship.

Solon's voyage gave him firsthand knowledge of the various roles of the personnel on the ship. Climbing the ropes involved successive promotion from the first assignment of cook's mate or deckhand to "ordinary," "able seaman," "idler," "second mate," "first mate," and finally captain. The ship's crew had well-defined work assignments. With each added responsibility and with more experience came the promise of more compensation. Boys worked hard at the docks and ship-yards to impress the crew and encourage them to hire them at a young age.

Boys, as young as ten, could be employed, typically their first job being cook's mate. As the youngster gained experience, he could take on the responsibilities of a fisherman and deckhand. The youths

TARRING ROPES.

often returned to their homes for additional schooling or to help with the farming or other family businesses after short voyages.

With some sailing experience, the deckhand or cook's mate would be promoted to "ordinary." The ordinary was a beginning sailor able to tie common knots, knowledgeable about the functions of riggings and capable of setting and furling sails, but still unqualified to do advance rigging maintenance or take the helm.

The "able seaman" was an experienced sailor, skilled in all manner of rigging maintenance. An able sailor was able to reef, furl, and set sail. He was also capable of sewing and running rigging. The able seaman was responsible for making "chafing gear," a rope encasement that prevented frictional wearing of the canvas sails. The able seaman also made many repairs to the equipment, rigging and sails.

The "idlers" or "specialists" filled the very specialized roles on the ships and were often expert sailors. They were housed in the steerage, aft of the main-post, in quarters better than seamen. Many sailors who developed highly specialized skills would fill these positions rather than climbing the ranks to become an officer. The carpenter maintained the woodwork, sealing the hatches and keeping seams watertight. The carpenter also maintained and repaired the mechanical systems, doing some blacksmithing. The

THE STEWARD.

sailmaker repaired shreds and tears in canvas and could sew ropes to the sails. The steward was responsible for the food supplies, busing the tables, and serving the captain. On larger passenger packets, the steward coordinated the activities of the waiters while seeing to the comfort of the passengers. The cook was housed in the galley and it was his duty to prepare food for everyone on board.

The officers had cabins in the stern. The second mate was responsible for the equipment in the boatswain's locker. His job was rough, no longer being one of the crew; the sailors treated him with disregard. Not quite an officer, he commanded no additional respect from officers who regarded him as just a sailor.

The first mate maintained the logbook. Being somewhat accountable to the ship's owners and insurers, he also had responsibility for the stowage, delivery and safety of the cargo. The *Sea-Man's Vade Mecum*, written in 1707, lists the duties of the first mate. He is responsible for the vessel's rigging, seeing that cables, anchors, sails, yards, and moorings were in good order or repaired while in port. He oversaw the anchor hoisted at departure. He executed the captain's orders and commanded the vessel in the absence or sickness of the captain.

IN HIS LETTER DATED NOVEMBER 17, 1850, SOLON DESCRIBES HIS ADVENTURES TO BATH, THEN ON TO HALLOWELL.

Hallowell Nov 17, 1850

My Dear Mother

we have arrived here safe at last we arrived at the mouth of the river Friday Morning in the afternoon we made sail and got up as far as Bath, where we anchord, in the morning we chased a schooner clear to Hallowell there is some talk of going to Vassalborough but I dont think I shall go for I believe the stage fare is very high our cook crippled himself this morning so that I had to make Bread for Dinner I cant think of anything to write but I will do the best I can Father is pretty well his leg has pained him some but not much I have had another chance to try Fathers shooting iron when we was down to the mouth of the river they were all down below but me a Cape Drake came flying by and I up gun and Dropped him you shall have the feathers fund upon it pa sends his best pair of specks to all the folks Give my love to Lucy J and Amey and all my Friends and save a good share For yourself give my best paire of specks to

RETRIEVING.

my Particular Friend

From Solon Hanson

SINCE PAPER WAS VERY EXPENSIVE, EVERY SCRAP WAS USED. ON THE BACK OF THE NOV 17, 1850 LETTER WAS A LIST OF ITEMS SOLD.

```
            Sold                              Sold

salt 94 bus @ $28.20              1 Bush Beans-9/ 1.50
3 1/2 bush Geite. 35 $1.22        2 Casks for Cider  9/1.50
5 quintls Cod fish 15.00          1 Bu-Cask        30¢
429 lbs dried apples @ 6¢ $25.74  5 Plaster Casks 100  1.00
10 bo Pollor    20.00             Hooping Casks     .50
4 barrals small mackerel 18.00    55 lbs. Cheese 8¢   4.40
1 bo Lary bo    10.00             239 lbs Butter 1/39.86
5 Bor Cod fish  18.00             Straw for apples    .25
1 bo Haddoc     3.00              8 Bar Apples      9.00
2 quinlts Hake  2.50              5 Bar—Cider 10/-  8.50
Wharfage 3.00                     50 lbs. Butter 18/6¢ 8.00
1 bar-beans 3.00
1 bar for Cider  .62
```

Note about weights and measures:

In the British Imperial System, a quintal or hundredweight is a measure of weight equal to 112 pounds. In the U.S. Customary System a hundred weight or "short hundred weight" is equal to 100 pounds. Today, a quintal is a metric unit of mass equal to 100 kilograms.

A bushel is a unit of volume typically used for dry measure. In U.S. Customary System, a bushel is equal to 4 pecks or 2,150.42 cubic inches. In the British Imperial System, a bushel is 2,219.36 cubic inches and is used for either dry or liquid measure.

A barrel is a unit of volume and its definition varies. In the U.S. Customary System, a barrel as a liquid measure is from 31 to 42 gallons as established by law or usage. A barrel may also be referred to as a "cask," a "bar," or a "Bo." "Bot" can also be an abbreviation for "butt" which is a large cask equal to 126 U.S. gallons.

LUCY NEWBERRY HANSON WROTE A LETTER CHOCK FULL OF PARENTAL ADVICE TO HER SON, SOLON, WHILE HE WAS ON A FISHING VOYAGE.

My Dear precious Solon

You cant conceive the pleasure I felt in reading your first letter. it was good and kind and just like my Sody. what a good boy you are to think so much of your poor Mother. I have felt very uneasy about you since you left home for fear you would be drowned. but I know Pa will learn you something every day and instill good principals into your well shaped head. I wish you could realize the difference between your Father and one that would hold the intoxicating bowl to your little lips or sow the seeds of vice in your tender heart.

Oh my Sody if you are as good as your Mother wishes you to be you will be a happy child, and a virtuous man. I hope you will always be an honor to your parents and be a pattern for Amos

Dear Solon

I am sick and tired. you must excuse this short letter and make haste home to the arms of your affectionate Mother

LNH

LECTURE ON SPIRITUALISM.

Chapter 5

GONE FISHING

S OLON'S FAMILY EXPERIENCED many adjustments in the early 1850s. The 1850 Penobscot census listed Solon's grandfather, Robert, age 66, as a farmer with real estate valued at $750, and his wife Sally (nickname for Sarah), age 64. Solon's sister, Lucy Jane, married Captain Francisco De Echenagucia on September 8, 1852. Shortly before, Lucy Jane had attended an academy of arts and sciences.

Castine had become a very crowded and busy place to live. In 1850, 500 of the vessels that fished the Grand Banks came to Castine to purchase needed equipment of salt, hooks, clothes, and rations. The shipyards continued to be productive, building, launching and repairing. In 1851, Stover P. Hatch and Moses Perkins built the 125-foot *Frances Hatch* with Masters Granville Springfield and John Gregory. The 162-foot *William Witherle* was built and subsequently sold in Hamburg and renamed *Selma*. The 161-foot *J. P. Whitney* and the 165-foot *Ostervald* were both launched in 1853. The *J. P. Whitney* was a square-rigger primarily owned by J. P. Whitney and Company of New Orleans, and partially owned by Castine fish partnerships with the Whitney firm.

Sometime around 1853, the Hanson family moved to a 30 acre farm in Penobscot about one mile up the Bagaduce River. Family records indicate that Solon and Amos helped with the farming. Captain Hanson probably found fishing provided as much satisfaction as it did remuneration. In a letter dated July 14, 1853, to his mother, Sarah, age 67, John Hanson described life at sea on a fishing voyage. The mention of "Pa and Frank" may refer to his father, then 70 years old, and Lucy Jane's husband Francisco (Frank) Echenagucia.

I suppose that pa and frank have got out to the West Indies before this time if they have had any kind of a passage.

This voyage took John from Castine to the narrow passage called the gut of Canso. Here, he conversed with the crews of the *Halifax*, the *George*, and other vessels. He spoke of his fishing berth, the assigned location on the ship's rail for manning his lines. His berth is second from the captain's, and it seems he is quite content.

The life of the Down East Grand Banks fishermen was both a battle with nature and with other fishermen. Before 1852 the fishermen may have witnessed serious international rivalry. The following excerpt from the *History of the United States*, by John Clark Ridpath, published by Jones Brothers and Company 1876, attests to the confrontational era:

> In 1852 a serious trouble arose with England. By the terms of former treaties the coast-fisheries of Newfoundland belonged exclusively to Great Britain. But outside of a line drawn three miles from the shore American fishermen enjoyed rights and privileges. Now the dispute arose as to whether the line should be drawn from one headland to another so as to give all bays and inlets to England, or whether it should be made to conform to the irregularities of the coast. Under the later construction American fishing-vessels would have equal claims in the bays and harbors; but this privilege was denied by Great Britain, and the quarrel rose to such a height that both nations sent men-of-war to the contested waters. But reason triumphed over passion, and in 1854 the difficulty was happily settled by negotiation; the right to take any fish in any part of the bays of the British possessions was conceded to American fishermen.

Although there are no direct references to Solon in the letters, the omission of John Hanson sending a greeting to Solon suggests that he may have been on this or some other voyage. The letters with Solon's papers do not tell the name of the ship or the captain that John Hanson fished with in 1853. On September 17, 1855, Charles K. Tilden wrote from Castine to Captain Francisco Echenagucia that Captain Hanson was with Captain Mullet in the Schooner *Sun,* engaged in fishing. Referring to the Grand Banks vessels, Mr. Tilden also wrote, "Our Bankers are coming in and have done quite fair." Captain Hanson seasonally fished with the Penobscot region Grand Banks fishermen.

IN A LETTER DATED JULY 14, 1853, JOHN HANSON DESCRIBES HIS FISHING
EXPEDITION TO HIS MOTHER, SARAH HUTCHINS HANSON.

July Thursday 14th 1853

My Dear Mother

we arrived in the gut of canso yesterday morning after being on the passage five days we left very sudden thursday night the cook had a terrible fuss he was what you might term drunk and wanted to leave the vessel but the captain kicked him over two or three times which cooled his courage very soon the English are having quite a time in the bay the Halifax has taken one American vessel for fishing within bounds there was an American Craft called the George came through the gut and four of her crew of darkies raised a mutiny the captain left them in the gut and the halifax took them up to port hood and put them in the Jug we have shipped two more men since we have been here one of them is John Mclane I have got a first rate fishing birth it is the second from the captain.

This paper is had what you might call a rum sweat it has laid in the bottom of bunk's chest and got a bottle of rum broke upon it however it will answer all purposes it is so dark down here that I cannot see whether the paper is ruled or not.

The crew are all first rate fellows ever one of them it is the first crew that ever I was with whare part of them was not drunk we have got a first rate vessel under foot and I think a good Mackerel Crew and if we can only light on thier heads we will fill her up in less than a month and be back again I hope their will be no strange thing found down to uncle bobs but I expect thare will before Augustus gets done haying. take good care of my old friend Leave and keep his noze clean.

I suppose that pa and frank have got out to the West Indies before this time if they have had any kind of a passage.

I shall send this home by the politeness of My Frederec Garland who came into the gut tonight they have got about 700 quintels of good cod fish but they have been gone long enough for them over four months.

I think it is about time to close give my love to capt Jerry Aunt Feeny and all the boys Lucy Jane and Amy tell Amy that he must not cry any more but go to farming give my love to all the Castine folks up to the big house in pidiculur so good bye for this time

from your dutiful Son
John L Hanson

Chapter 6

SOLON AS A COASTAL FISHERMAN

I N THE MID 1850S, the business of fishing involved not only families but also communities. The fishing vessels could be community properties owned by entire villages where each family had a responsibility, owning a share in them and their enterprises. Occasionally, a fisherman gained ownership of a vessel or a fleet of half a dozen vessels. In 1854, investors in Castine launched the 184-foot *Samuel Adams* and the 172-foot *Benjamin Thaxter.*

The fishing expeditions usually lasted from three to five months. Each vessel required a crew of eight to ten men and boys. The boys started out as cook's mates, and with experience became fishermen and deckhands. The boys were known as "cut-tails" since they used pieces of the fish tails as evidence of the quantity they caught and were paid accordingly. The "tars" (short for tarpaulin, another word for sailor) worked when the fish were running. The crews of vessels from Maine were, as in Solon's letter, often referred to as "cow yard tars," a nickname for men and boys who fished when the opportunity arose in order to support their small farms. A boy from Castine might have been a farmer, lumberman, fisherman, deckhand, and work for hire in many other specialized fields before his eighteenth birthday.

Successful fishermen developed a complete understanding of the nature of the fish. Knowledge of fish habits, weather, and currents were important for locating fish. The fish harvested were typically from one of two fish families: the cod, family Gadidae, and the mackerel, family Scombridae.

47

Mackerels are found in tropical or temperate seas. The mackerel family includes chub mackerel, Atlantic mackerel, tuna and albacore. While most mackerel species stay in the ocean, some come into the bays where they are important for coastal and shore fishing. These fish are eaten fresh or canned since their blood-rich bodies spoil quickly and, if eaten spoiled, cause scombroid food poisoning. The chub mackerel and the Atlantic mackerel can be identified by the striped pattern of dozens of

Mackerel

blackish, near vertical, wavy bars across the body. The term "mackerel sky" (refering to striations of cirrocumulus clouds that indicate precipitation within 24 hours) arose from the cloud systems having patterns similar to the markings on the mackerel.

Fishing was mainly done by hand-lining. The Maine coastline produced cod, mackerel, halibut, haddock, hake, blue and occasionally a dolphin. Most fish taken were cod unless mackerel were found. Fishing for mackerel, a more elusive fish swimming near the surface in schools, was a less lucrative pursuit, though easier than cod fishing. A typical four-month voyage would haul roughly 30,000 fish.

Fishing voyages were easier to manage than trade voyages as the men could often row ashore for fresh water or to hunt game. The forests in Maine are populated with white-tailed deer, turkey, grouse, partridge, rabbit, moose and other game. Along the shores, they could harvest waterfowl. The hunters carried muskets, bullets and powder horns. A powder horn is a convenient, hermetic container for carrying gunpowder. Hunters fashioned them from cow and ox horns. The horns were about fifteen to eighteen centimeters long, outfitted with a plug at one end and a cap at the other. The outside of the horn was often scrimshawed, a form of decorative carving. With access to the coast for fresh water and food, fewer provisions were needed on board and the diet was better.

On April 16, 1854, Solon wrote from Little Deer Isle to his mother. This expedition might have been to harvest cod or mackerel. The Asa Howard he refers to may have been his neighbor; the "A. Howard" listed as residing on Water Street, north of Dyer Lane, on the 1860 map in the *Castine Visitor,* Spring 1998.

On November 26, 1854, Solon wrote from Millbridge to his mother that they were almost loaded and ready to sail at the end of the week. Millbridge had specialized in smoking herring and in building ships.

Solon mentioned a hunting accident in Cherryfield, a town upriver from Millbridge. The crew had left Solon, Asa Howard, and the cook aboard, and went hunting. One hunter mistook a fellow crewmember for a deer and shot him through the chest.

When not working, the seamen were packed into the forecastle, the superstructure at the bow of the ship. The following description of life in the forecastle was published in 1846 by political reporter J. Ross Brown, who experienced this life firsthand. It was subsequently published in *American Maritime Heritage* by Engle and Lott:

> It would be difficult to give any idea of our forecastle. In wet weather, when most of the hands were below, cursing, smoking, singing, and spinning yarns, it was perfect bedlam. Think of three or four Portuguese, a couple Irishmen, five or six rough Americans, in a hole about sixteen feet wide . . . so low that a full grown person could not stand upright in it, and so wedged with the rubbish as to leave scarcely room for a foothold. It contained twelve small berths, and with fourteen chests in the little area around the ladder, seldom admitted to being clean. In warm weather, it was insufferable close. It would seem like exaggeration to say, that I have seen in Kentucky pig-sties not half as filthy, and in every respect preferable to this miserable hole; such however is the fact.

Solon reported that many of the crew left and the forecastle was quite cold in November when the salt water along the coastline is freezing cold.

> we have only one man before the mast besides me and he went home yesterday so I am alone in my glory with three officers all to myself. I suffered like the devil in that cold snap for we have no stove in the forecastle and was at work in the water almost all the time and it would freeze any where it strike but things are a little

better now we have a first rate stove in the forecastle and
the weather is quite moderate.

Although Solon didn't write about any of the stories or "yarns" the
crew told on this excursion, local lore and family stories suggest that
there were stories about ghosts and sea monsters. In Castine, two ghost
stories originating during the American Revolution survive to this day.
One is recorded in George Wheeler's book, *History of Castine, Penobscot,
and Brooksville*. George Wheeler was a contemporary of Solon. The story
was part of William Hutchings' "Narrative of the Siege," as told to Mr.
Joseph L. Stevens, Jr. in August of 1855. William Hutchings was 15 years
old at the time of the expedition. He fled with his family after the British
destroyed the American fleet. He served in the Massachusetts Regiment
during the war. The British landed on June 1, 1779, in front of Joseph L.
Perkins' house on what is now the southeast corner of Main and Water
Streets. The confrontation between the British and Americans involved
bloody battles, the climax of which was the famous Penobscot Expedition. Hutchings relates:

> I recollect seeing some of the American fleet drop in
> behind Nautilus Island and fire across the bar at the
> English ships. Their last shot ploughed up dry sod
> near Hatch's house, and set considerable of it on fire.
> A drummer was killed, the night of the skirmish, at the
> battery near Bank's house, and for a good many years
> after, people used to say that they could hear his ghost
> drumming there at midnight.

When the war was over, the family returned to Penobscot and Hutchings worked as farmer, lumberman, and in the coastal trade. He lived to
be 100 years old, making him Maine's last Revolutionary soldier. William Hutchings was the oldest brother of Sarah Hutchins, who married
Robert Hanson and was Solon's grandmother. Some of the children of
Charles Hutchins and Mary Perkins had names recorded as Hutchings
and others were recorded as Hutchins. More about his life is written
in the article "William Hutchins and the American Revolution," *Wilson
Museum Bulletin*, Castine, Maine, Winter 1984.

Legend has it that another drummer boy was said to have been held in the prison at Fort George. The British captured a number of Americans during the Penobscot Expedition. The Americans planned an escape for the very next rainy, foggy night. When they were escaping, the drummer boy was asleep, and the soldiers were unable to rouse him. Soon after this, the British abandoned the prison, forgetting to take him along. His skeleton was discovered years later with his hands still grasping the drumsticks. It is said that his ghost marches down Perkins Street drumming loudly on a foggy night in August.

Gigantic sea creatures were also a popular topic among the seamen. *Harper's New Monthly Magazine* documents one of the local stories. In 1809, a Reverend Abraham Cummings claimed to have seen a sea-serpent in the Penobscot Bay while he was in a boat with his wife, daughter, and another lady. He estimated it was about 60 feet long, and as thick as a sloop's mast. Apparently, from 1770, various persons, fishermen, shoremen, and the British reported sighting animals of the same description along the eastern coast of America.

THE GREAT SEA-SERPENT, ACCORDING TO BISHOP PONTOPPIDAN.

IN HIS LETTER DATED APRIL 16, 1854 TO HIS MOTHER, SOLON REPORTS THAT THEIR SHIP WAS AT LITTLE DEER ISLE, MAINE.

Little Deer Isle

Tuesday, April 16, 1854

My Dear Mother,

We arrived here last friday evening and have laid here ever since we are now all ready to sail as soon as the skipper comes on board we expect him to come aboard this afternoon we have had a first rate time since we have laid here,

the crew is all gone ashore but the cook and me and Asa Howard who is
asleep on the main Hatch he has just getting over a fortnight drunk. I write
you this in great haste for I have got two go to work and fix my lines give my
love to all the folks tell Amy to kiss Frone for me.
    So good bye

Yours,
Solon J. Hanson

**A LETTER DATED NOVEMBER 26, 1854 FROM SOLON HANSON AT
MILLBRIDGE TO HIS MOTHER.**

Milbridge Sun Nov 26–54

Dear Mother

*We are now almost loaded and probably shall be ready to sail by the last of
this week we are all well as ever I have a d_d bad pen as my writing will
testify.*
    *we have been at work all this week night and day towing down rafts
when we could and at work on board whether we could or not on one of
our crew left last friday but he was an irishman and so it was not of much
account. we got your letter last tuesday and was very glad to hear that Mr.
Cate wanted old munt but dont you let him have her pa laffed very much
about it. we have only one man before the mast besides me and he went
home yesterday so I am alone in my glory with three officers all to myself.*
    *I forgot to mention a very slight accident that happened in cherryfield
about ten days ago there was a party of men went out in the woods and
carried a powder horn apiece. they parted and agreed to meet in a field one
of them getting there first sat down in a little clump of bushes and the next
one that come up took him for a deer and rested over a rock about 25 yards
off let drive at him the ball went in his right breast and come out alongside
his back bone he yelled so as to be heard a mile and a half they carried him
home and he is now getting well you must not let ame carry the powder
horn in the woods any more all this helps to spill up.*
    *I suffered like the devil in that cold snap for we have no stove in the
forecastle and was at work in the water almost all the time and it would*

freeze any where it strike but things are a little better now we have a first rate stove in the forecastle and the weather is quite moderate.

we have got the dog again and pa has concluded to bring him home he is such a propper handy critter about the ship I stopped at Capt Eaton's all night when I was in Castine Cad is going to give me her dogtype when I get back that is rich I have not received any letter from jed Freathy yet and I dont know what to make of it I should thought he would have wrote.

Give my love to all the boys an girls that think enogh about me to inquire about me. tell Horatho that we wish he was here for we have only two for a crew I shall try to get this letter in the office today if I can I dont suppose it will be of any use to answer this I have not received any answer to the other one I wrote Give my love to Lucy Jane Ame and Hermy and save a large piece for yourself. having no more room I shall have to close so good bye

Solon Hanson himself

Lucy Jane Hanson with her son Herman Echenagucia

Chapter 7

CAPTAIN FRANCISCO DE ECHENAGUCIA

L UCY JANE CONTINUED her studies past grammar school. An inscription in her handwriting, inside her Latin Dictionary reads "Miss Lucy Jane Hanson at W Hunts Academy of the arts and sciences June 24, 1851." Families involved in the merchant marine industry often sent their daughters away to school in Boston and their sons to sea by their teen years. It is possible she met Francisco De Echenagucia while away at school. Captain De Echenagucia was born January 29, 1829, in St. Sebastian, Spain, on the Bay of Biscay. As a sea captain, he probably made port in Boston. On September 8, 1852, he and Lucy Jane were married in a ceremony performed by Charles Tilden, Esq., a neighbor and family friend often mentioned in these letters.

On July 30, 1853, Herman Echenagucia was born, while his grandfather Captain John Hanson was on a fishing voyage. The event was recorded in the family Bible: "Herman Hahn Echenagucia, born Penobscot July 30, 1853, Sunday morn at 4 o'clock." Solon referred to him as Hermey or Hermy. Lucy Jane spent most of her days farming and earned extra money by churning butter.

From the Solon papers cache, the following correspondence of Francisco relayed information about the building of the vessels and trade. On December 31, 1853, a contract was written that Tilden and Smith, both of Cherryfield, would build a Hermaphrodite Brig for Capt. Francis Echenagucia.

William Hutchinson Rowe wrote about the shipyards in his book, *Maritime History of Maine*. The smaller yards, like Cherryfield, employed between twenty to thirty men and built a schooner a year. Rowe described the region surrounding Cherryfield:

> Finally there is the coast east of the Penobscot, which was especially the home of the small schooner. Of the 1,990 vessels registered in the District of Machias, 1,550 were fore-and-afters . . . As always, the rivers play their part—the Union with Ellsworth, the Narraguagas with Millbridge and Cherryfield, the Harrington with the little town of that name. Here in 1856 the yards gave work to eighteen master builders, and there were as many as eight vessels on the stocks at one time. Between the bays of Harrington and Machias, which is a distance of but twenty miles, there are nine rivers which gave access to rich forests of spruce and pine.

The classification of sailing vessels is based on spars, rigging and to some extent on the hull shape. Some description of the component parts of the sailing vessels is necessary before it can be classified. A spar is a rigid stick designed to hold a sail. The vertical spars are called masts. Horizontal spars that cross a mast are called yards, while horizontal spars that are anchored at one end to the mast and extend to the foot of a sail are called booms. The angled spars which support the top of a sail are called gaffs. Between these spars, many types of sails can be fitted. The basic sail shapes are square and truncated triangular. Different combinations of rigging, masts, and hull shapes are classified as nine principal types of American sailing vessels: sloop, full-rigged brig, hermaphrodite brig, brigantine, top sail schooner, schooner, bark, tall ship, and barkentine.

The contract between Lucy Jane's husband, Francisco De Echenagucia, and Tilden and Smith specified that the cost would be $32 per ton,

Sloop   *Full Rigged Brig*   *Hermaphrodite Brig*   *Brigantine*   *Top Sail Schooner*

with the vessel being about 275 tons. Specifications for the hermaphrodite brig were given:

> The Frame to be of hard Wood and Hacmetac Wales to
> be of Oak—plank under the Wales to be of Hard Wood
> Beams to be of Norway Pine—Hacmetac Knees White
> Pine Deck—Hacmetac & Beech Treenaies—Clamps to
> be Hacmetac and Norway Pine—Thick Streaks to be
> Hard Woods—Ceiling to be of Norway and Spruce—
> to be fastened with Composition Spikes & Butt bolted
> with Copper—Her Bilge Boles to be driven through the
> Timbers upon the outsides before Planking said vessel
> to have a patent Windlass—The Cabins to be on deck
> also a House for the Men—The Hull to be painted with
> Three coats of Paints inboard and outboard, & the Spars
> with two coats.

On April 28, 1854, George F. Tilden wrote of the progress their Pine Sails shipyard had made so far. The shipyard was employing fifteen men.

> In regard to the vessel, I am able to inform you that her
> frames are all up and that she is nearly all timbered out
> forward and aft. [The vessel] would have been entirely
> [built], but for some stormy days when the men could
> not work.

The vessel under construction was larger than they had originally planned and would make a good bark.

> Some of our Captains say she would make a fine Bark
> and no doubt she would; but of course you are to say

Schooner   *Bark*   *Tall Ship*   *Barkentine*

with the other owners whether any change shall be made in the rig or not. If desired, we are willing to fit her for a Bark, but must know very soon . . . As the vessel is larger than at first talked of, we shall put in the hanging knees; which will add much to her strength. This we do aside from the contract, and if the owners feel disposed to allow us anything for it, they can do so.

In Griffith's *Ship-Builder's Manual*, 1856, within a discussion of the science of mast and spar making, the "force of propulsory power" of masts and spars is explained. Griffith lists the proportions needed and the significance of using the proper tree wood for masts. The mainmast of a ship or a brig was supposed to be one inch in diameter for every three feet in length, whereas the masts of a cutter or schooner were to be one fourth of an inch in diameter for each foot in length. Other masts had proportions relative to the mainmast. When selecting wood, the strength, weight, and function were of prime importance. The yardarms had to sustain the forces of a fully furled sail sometimes under extreme wind conditions. In Griffith's words, "the proportions that give strength to a spar will at the same time endow it with the elements of beauty."

The vessel is rigged as a bark and launched as the *John Wesley*. Francisco Echenagucia was a part owner and the original captain of the ship. The saga told through these letters describes Francisco's adventures as a captain aboard the *John Wesley*. Business at the time was becoming difficult with the approach of the Civil War and the strained trade abroad due to international problems such as the French Revolution. Francisco became ill and his financial stresses were mounting. Sadly, he did not recover. Francisco died January 23, 1856, six days before his 28th birthday. He is buried in the Castine cemetery.

Lucy Jane Hanson Echenagucia married Captain John Foster Peterson on May 23, 1859. Together Lucy and John had five children: Helen Martha, Solon Hanson, Kate Paxton, Harold and Joseph. Helen married Fred Morton Conner. Helen and Fred had two sons, Everett and Edwin Solon Conner. The story of John Peterson's life is recorded in the *Bangor Daily News*, September 12, 1907. After serving as mate on the *U.S.S. Flambeau*, the *U.S.S. Chatham* and the *U.S.S. Laburnum* during the Civil War, he became a well-known captain in the schooner fishing fleet. The *Bucksport Herald*, Friday, September 23, 1898, reports that he captained the *A.V.S. Woodruff* to bring home a record-breaking Grand Banks fishing expedition with 300 tons of Cod. The *Bucksport Herald* reported that this was a world record for the cargo which was "without doubt the largest ever brought from the Grand Banks into an American port."

Lucy Jane's farmhouse in Penobscot

A CONTRACT FOR TILDEN & SMITH TO BUILD A VESSEL FOR ECHENAGUCIA WAS DATED DECEMBER 31, 1853.

Copy

This memo Made this Thirty First Day of December AD One Thousand Eight Hundred and Fifty Three by Geo. F. Tilden and Talbot Smith both of Cherryfield in the County of Washington, State of Maine.

Witnesseth

That said Tilden & Smith hereby agree to build a vessel in said Cherryfield of about Two Hundred Seventy Five Tons Burthen—said vessel to be a Hermaphrodite Brig, and to be built as follows. To wit—The Frame to be of hard Wood and Hacmmetac Wales to be of Oak—plank under the Wales to be of Hard Wood Beams to be of Norway Pine.—Hacmetac Knees White Pine Deck—Hacmetac & Beech Treenaies—Clamps to be Hacametac and Norway Pine—Thick Streaks to be Hard Woods—Ceiling to be of Norway and Spruce—to be fastened with Composition Spikes & Butt bolted with Copper.—Her Bilge Boles to be driven through the Timbers upon the outside before Planking said vessel to have a patent Windlass—The Cabins to be on deck also a House for the Men—The Hull to be painted with Three coats of Paints inboard and outboard, & the Spars with two coats—And the said Tilden & Smith further agree that said vessel, meaning the Hule Spars shall be built at their ship yard Pine Sails Cherryfield in a thorough, faithful & Workmanlike manner, & that she shall be completed & and launched by them in all the Month of July, One Thousand Eight Hundred & Fifty Four & that they will build said vessell for, and at the rate of Thirty two dollars per ton—said vessel shall be owned in such proportions as the parties who may hereafter subscribe to this agreement may set against their names.—Payment for the same to be made as follows—viz—One Quarter part when the vessel shall be set up—One Quarter part when she is launched: and notes to be given for the balance at Three & six months with interest from the time the vessel is launched—It is understood that said vessel shall be Iron fastened in all respects except as specified in the body of this agreement

Ive witness whereof the Parties have hereunto set and subscribed their names the day and year before written.

A LETTER, DATED APRIL 28, 1854, FROM GEORGE F. TILDEN IN CHERRYFIELD TO ECHENAGUCIA DESCRIBES PROGRESS ON BUILDING THE BARK.

Cherryfield April 28th 1854

Capt. Francis Echanaguicia

Dear Sir

I presume you think it about time to hear something in regard to the vessel now being built for you—Since my return here I have been exceedingly busy & further past week have been confined to the house by sickness. Sever cold & sore throat has been my trouble—No doubt you can sympathize with those who are sick, as you have had so much experience the past year yourself. In regard to the vessel, I am able to inform you that her frames are all up & that she is nearly all timbered out forward & aft; Would have been entirely, but for some stormy days when the men could not work. We have got a first rate frame—as good as any we set up here & am going along well with the work—have some fifteen men employed in the yard—The vessel I think from present appearance will measure over 300 Tons—Some of our Capts say she would make a fine Bark & no doubt she would; but of course you are to say with the other owners whether any change shall be made in the rig or not—I have written to Father in regard to this matter today & should be glad to have you see him as soon after you receive this as possible. If desired, we are willing fit her for a Bark, but must know very soon. As the vessel is larger than at first talked of, we shall put in hanging knees; which will add much to her strength—This we do aside from the contract, & if the owners feel disposed to allow us anything for it, they can do so,—Should like to see you here in course of a fortnight so that you can instruct our master workmen in regard to planning the cabins—By some mishap we seemed to miss seeing each other when I was last at Castine, I called at your house on my way here, but was informed that you had gone to Castine to see me. Although I had nothing particular to say, Yet I should have been pleased to see you; Hope your health continues to improve—Please let me hear from you soon

Very Truly Your Friend
Geo. F. Tilden

A LETTER WRITEN TO ECHENAGUCIA DATED SEPTEMBER 17, 1855, FROM CHARLES K. TILDEN IN CASTINE WROTE ABOUT THE DIFFICULTIES IN NEW ORLEANS, AND ACTIVITIES BACK HOME.

Castine Sept 17/55

Capt. F. Echenagucia

> *My Dear Sir,*

By the inclos'd under date of June 14th you will presume that three months have passed since I wrote you, and Bad to relate, that letter has remained in my possession the day I intended to have mail'd that letter, I rec' information from Capt. Perkins which lead me to believe you would have left Cadiz before my letter could have reach'd you---I rec' by late mail information from Capt. Perkins, that you would probably arrive at N Orleans about the last of this month—should no accident befall you and your health be good, I think this change in your Destination may prove for the interest of the Bark—this expectation I sincerley hope may be realiz'd as much for my welfare, depend on the favourable operation of your good self and the good Bark "John Wesley." since visiting, under date of June

14/ [illegible] *I have had the pleasure of a letter from Mr.* [Brnfusan?] *of Cadiz on the subject of salt—he writes me quite to the point and I have repl'd asking information as to the facilities for obtaining a cargo in the Spring—shall most likely hear from Mr. B. soon I shall enclose a copy of his letter—you will here permit me to thank you for your prompt and particular attention to my wishes—In all this salt business, I repeat, That I am not so anxious to carry it out, as to have it draw the vessel off from most productive business—the rate information from N Orleans is of character to hold out the expectation of good business for all vessels—this expectations I trust may be realized and sincerely hope you may be so fortunate as to secure operation of the best there is going forward—in all cases, My Dear Sir, permit me to caution you to be very carefull as to your health—do not expesc yourself unnecessarily—N. Orleans, you are undoubted is* [illegible] *is one of the most (if not the very worst) expensive Ports in the world—the ultimate prudence & caution is requir'd—please excuse me, Capt if in my anxiety for the success of your voyage I should urge the principles of Econo—my somewhat earnestly—much, very much depends on watchfullness in every branch, for the interest of your voyage—affairs at home have not chang'd much since you left home—your friends are all well—Capt. Hanson is with Capt. Mullet in the Sch. Sun, engaged fishing—our Bankers are coming in and have done quite fair—Capt. John Gardner—in the Sch. Darreynapes (Captain Cornwallis having left) is in his scond voyage to the West Indies—Capt. Cornwallis is about to take command (having been at home all summer) if a new Brig, Building in Surry, in which he takes a small interest—Capt. C. Bryant has not been to sea since his return to N York—he is in a visit with his wife at Bucksport, quite unwell—I fear for his recovery—Capt. Eaton is on a fishing voyage—Mr Noyes has commenc'd building a ship of about 1000 tons—another of the same size is expected to be put up on the Jarvis yard—but not by the Jarvis'—The Steamer Secer has been running this summer—will probably haul off next month—we expect to have a Telegraph line built between this time and first of Nov.—many other matters & things may occur in time ____ please let me hear from you at the earliest period, writing fully & freely allow me again to say, be careful of your health truly yr. fr.*

Charles K. Tilden

Son Geo. is at Cherryfield, try to close up bad business.

A LETTER DATED SEPTEMBER 28, 1855 TO ECHENEGUCIA ON THE BARK *John Wesley* IN NEW ORLEANS, FROM JOSEPH PERKINS IN NEW YORK EXPRESSES HOPE FOR SECURING GOOD BUSINESS TO TRAVEL BACK NORTH.

New York Sept 28th 1855

Capt. Frances De Echenegucia

Bark Jno Wesley

New Orleans

Dear Sir

I wrote you last under date of 5th inst care of J. H. Bass. Esqu and since then have been in some doubt as to your being ordered to New Orleans as Mr. Saportas has not rec'd any letters from his agents at Res mentioning your destination and receiving the letter enclosed from the East still strengthened my doubts I have however learned to day from pretty good authority that you are bound there and have therefore continued to write you and send the enclosed letter—I hope you will be able to get good business from there to the North as coastwise frieghts by last accts were high I have nothing new to write you and referring you to my former letter

I remain

yours truly

Joseph Perkins

A LETTER DATED OCTOBER 31, 1855, FROM JOSEPH PERKINS IN NEW YORK TO ECHENAGUCIA IN CASTINE RECORDED THE FACT THAT ECHENAGUCIA WAS ILL.

New York October 31st 1855

Capt. Frances De Echnegucia

Castine

Dear Sir—

Herewith I hand you letter received this morning which I presume by stamp is from Mess. J. P. Whitney Co. I hope you arrived home safe and after a little quiet together with good nursing I flatter myself you will be fully restored to your usual good health—I should be pleased to hear from

you at anytime and hope you will write me how you progress in your recov-
ery as I look upon the event as a certainty—I flatter myself that you will
explain matters satisfactorily to Mess. Tilden and Son concerning your voy-
age and that they will be convinced that you have used your best endeavours
for the benefit of all concerned I shall look for the Barks arrival here in the
course of ten or twelve days. and presume that George will come on—I have
nothing further to add and with my best wishes for your speedy recovery
                    I remain

                         Your friend
                         Joseph Perkins

A NOTE OF SETTLEMENT DATED DEC. 1855 FROM JOSEPH PERKINS.

Capt. F. Echenagucia
1855   to Joseph Perkins Sr.
May 15 To Postage on Letters to Cadiz   .92
Nov. 10 " sight drft   147.32
Dec. 5   " do-do for George F. Tilden   91.55
          " Balance fwd George F. Tilden   53.78
                                              $293.57
1855   Credit
Apr 30 By Cash   60.70
July 16 " do   225.00
Dec 5   Interest to date (balance)   7.78
                                              $293.57
    NewYork Dec. 5, 1855
                              Settled
                              Joseph Perkins
    53.98   per H. Saunduson

A MEMORANDUM OF AGREEMENT DATED SEPTEMBER 1, 1856 FROM JOHN
HANSON RECORDED THE SALE OF ECHENAGUCIA'S SHARE OF THE BARK.

(Duplicated)
Castine Sept. 1st 1856
This mendm of agreement made the day and year above written
Witnesseth
          That John Hanson, Mariner, of Penobscot, as
administrator of the estate of Capt. Francis D. Echenagucia, deseased, hereby

bargins and sells unto Geo. F. Tilden, of Castine, Merchant, One Eigth part of the Bark "John Wesley," the same being apart of the Estate of said Echenagucia for the sum of one Thousand Dollars, the said Eigth to be conveyed to said Tilden by a good and sufficient Bill of Sale Whereon said Tilden shall give his notes, Endorsed by Capt. Joseph Perkins, of New york or any other person who may be satisfactory to said Hanson as follows—

One note for Five Hundred Dollars payable to Isacue Grindle or order, in one year from date with interest, One note for four Hundred Dollars payable to Mrs. Lucy J. Echenagucia on demand, with interest, (the payment of which is not to be demanded within one year from date). Also One hundred Dollars to be paid said Hanson in cash when called for_

John Hanson

Witness
Otis Little

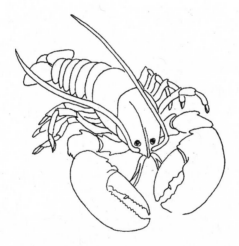

Referred to as bugs by Down East fishermen, lobsters were plentiful from Colonial times through the 1800s. Colonial children waded the low tide shore gathering five- to ten-pound lobsters among the rocks, enough to feed several families. Perhaps because of taboos having Biblical origins, some families felt shame, and buried the shells so no one would know. According to Colin Woodard, lobsters were fed to prisoners and indentured servants, and one group in Massachusetts took owners to court, winning a ruling that they would not be served lobster more than three times a week. In 1850, lobsters were primarily bait; by 1880 the $430,000 lobster industry was the 4th largest commercial fish industry.

Castine

New Orleans

Chapter 8

TO NEW ORLEANS

B Y AGE 17, SOLON had established himself as an ordinary seaman. The responsibilities of farming in the late spring through summer and fishing the Grand Banks in the fall left him enough time each winter to embark on one or possibly two trade voyages along the coast. In the winter of 1855, he took a position with Captain Chase sailing a bark on a trade mission from Blue Hill, Maine, to New Orleans, Louisiana. Solon's adventure on this trip is documented in three letters he sent home from New Orleans while waiting for their cargo of cotton.

In the 1850s, triangle trade routes were established to export New England products from Boston to New Orleans and southern crops to foreign ports. The first routes were orchestrated by Boston investors who traded abroad in order to import foreign goods. Maine entrepreneurs were able to enter triangle trade with New Orleans and foreign ports due to their success in fishing. Maine exported fish and timber to southern states. By the 1850s, Penobscot and New Orleans investors formed alliances that circumvented and competed with Boston traders.

In *Fifty Years of Fortitude*, Kendrick Daggett described three general classifications of merchant marine: the tramps, the regular traders, and the packets. The tramps were transients that traveled to any port with no schedule or fixed route. The cargo for the next voyage was whatever profitable trade business the captain could secure while delivering the last cargo. "Bully" captains and "bucko" mates often operated the tramps. Sometimes the crews were physically and verbally mistreated, underfed, sleep deprived, and underpaid. In contrast, the regular traders maintained flexible, predictable, seasonal trading patterns with stable business contacts gained through reputation. The regular traders operated like independent teamsters, and had a choice of a trading voyage, fishing trip, or staying home to farm. The packets had regular routes on fixed time schedules to predetermined ports.

By Daggett's definition of tramps, traders, and packets, and by Solon's description of his situation, Solon must have been sailing on a tramp. Solon's mates and captain have rather objectionable personalities:

> The captain is the most snappish little cur I ever saw or heard of yet.
>
> The second mate is a regular tobacco mill, always with a tear on the end of his nose like a trailing rat. I was his second choice. We washed our figurehead and cutwater off the first blow.
>
> As soon as we struck the levee two of our crew left, and Sam and I left the next day. We are both at a private house.

After battling the weather around the Nantucket Shoals and suffering illnesses, most of the crew deserted the bark in New Orleans. However, jobs were hard to come by, and in the end many of them returned for the next trip.

An understanding of the daily schedule on a sailing vessel may shed some light into why sailors deserted. Sailing vessels maintained clockwork daily schedules. The day was divided into five four-hour watches, and two two-hour watches.

Before departing, the crew was assembled to assign each member to a watch. The first mate selected the port watch with the chores of maintaining the port side, the foremast canvas, and all the equipment between the foremast and the bow. The second mate selected the starboard watch with the responsibilities of maintaining the starboard side, and equipment between the stern and the foremast.

The process of dividing the crew was like picking teams in a high school gym class. The first mate had first choice, and then the second mate chose his favorite. The first mate chose a third from the remaining. The mates alternated until all crew assignments were complete. Like high school teams, there was considerable rivalry. The order of selection established something of a pecking order among the sailors. Being first selected distinguished a sailor as being quite capable of quality seamanship.

Following the cycle of watches, sailors had four hours of duty followed by four hours of rest. The odd number of watches allowed sailors to have the same schedule every other day, and to have responsibilities during all watches.

The schedule worked fine for moderate weather and sea conditions. Changes in weather, equipment failure and other factors, such as a serious error in navigation, could lead to "all hands" required during a watch. The crew was prepared for this, and eventually the system recovered. When unforeseen complications arose that required all-hands watches over a period of days or when a significant portion of the crew became ill and could not keep their watches, the system broke. Sleep deprivation led to fighting, sloppy seamanship, and additional illness. The schedule prohibited any long sequence of interruptions. A rough passage, inexperienced sailors, understaffing due to illness, and conflicting personalities living in close quarters put a lot of pressure on the sailors. At the journey's end, the captains of tramps often enlisted the sailors when they were short of dockworkers for unloading, loading and repairing at port. Under pressure, the sailors found relief by proclaiming their freedom and walking away from the situation.

Solon indicated that the stress level was high when they reached New Orleans. The crew had experienced a rough 26-day passage:

> After we left and come very near loosing her on Nantucket shoals we were in the breakers before we knew it but we got clear bless God.

According to *The Elements of Sailmaking: A Dictionary of Technical Terms Relative to Sails*, written by Robert Kipping in 1847, a close-reef means "The fourth or lowest reef of a topsail, and uppermost reef of a fore-and-aft mainsail." Reefing is the process of shortening a set sail to decrease the area, and hence the power delivered by the wind. The term "close-reefed" indicates that all the reefs of the topsails are taken in. Solon mentioned, "we never had nothing but close reefed topsails." This reference provides an indication of the weather, considering the speed of their passage. Solon reports the drama of a crew member:

[He was] lee easing reefing the mainsail and she rolled
so as to touch his feet in the water. I have heard of vessels soiling their yard arms in the water, but that was
coming the nearest that ever I want to see it.

The phrase "lee easing reefing" means that he was reefing a sail that
was perpendicular to the wind. The experience underscores the complexity of sailing.

Furling, and setting sails on a superficial level seem elementary. Furling is the process of folding the sail into a neat, controllable roll secured
to jackstays of the yard. The sailors would, in sequence, lower the yard,
haul in the clewlines to fold the sail in half, haul in the leechlines to fold
over the corners, and haul in the buntlines to pleat folds in the sail. Then
the sailors would tightrope walk across the yard and position themselves
in set intervals along the yard to secure the folded sail in the jackstays and
then lash it to the yard.

Setting sail is the reverse process, where the yards are lowered and the
sails unfolded. The mechanics of furling, setting, and reefing a single sail
are easily grasped. Innovations during the Industrial Revolution reduced
the work force and the individual prowess required.

The complexity comes from the interactions of booms and yards on
different masts and from weather conditions. The mates defined the sequence of sails to be set or furled and the orientations of the yards and
booms so that they would not tangle or tip the vessel. The sailors needed
to pay close attention to these orders and to keep the ropes oriented in
their proper locations. It takes many years of experience under different
weather conditions, in different currents, and in different coastal envi-
ronments to acquire the knowledge required to fully understand these
sequences.

IN HIS LETTER DATED FEBRUARY 18, 1855, SOLON DESCRIBES THEIR
PASSAGE FROM BLUE HILL, MAINE, TO NEW ORLEANS, LOUISIANA.

New Orleans Sun Feb 18. 1855

My Dear Mother

we arrived here last thursday after a rough passage of 26 days from blue hill we took a gale of wind the monday after we left and come very near loosing her on Nantucket shoals we were in the breakers before we knew it but we got clear bless God

we never had nothing but close reefed topsails on her from that time till we got into the gulf we anchored two nights on the bahama's. made the light on the balize and run for it till we run ashore and was towed up town by the steamer Yankee.

the captain is the most snappish little cur I ever saw or heard of yet it was nothing but kicks and cuffs with poor sam as soon as we struck the levee two of our crew left and sam and I left the next day we are both at a private house. the triangle exchange front Levee street Capt Lufkin is here in his new ship there is no chances to go north I dont know but I shall have to go back on board the bark again I would give all my old boots if I was at home for this city is the worst place that ever was made yet nothing but fighting all the time.

Horace Varnum the mate want me to come back but I dont want to work on them socks [sacks] you know that the captain said that the crew would have nothing to do with the onloading now he wants the crew to work in the hold and hot enough to roast the devil Sam keep's about half drunk all the time it is no use my talking to him if he dont stop it I shant stay by him much longer I shall endeavor to get home as quick as I can If I can find a ship bound on to the north I shall work my passage if I cant ship no other way

I have received no letters from home yet I dont know wheather you have wrote any or not but I suppose not for all the crew but I and sam I have hardly any thing more to say except that I hope you are all well Give my love to all the folks at home kiss the baby for me tell Amy to stick at home like the devil as soon as I get a chance to come home I will let you know

I have but very little money coming to me you know father got ten dollars advance for me and I got some clothes so you can see I am hard up not having a cent now I have not seen the captain since I left and he aint going to give me but

[paper torn, illegible] a month but dam the [paper torn] theare is plenty of ships on the levee and no man starves in this country I will come home as quick as I can so dont fret nor worry about me I have nothing more to write Give my love to all from your Son Solon Hanson

In Solon's sheltered childhood, he enjoyed the privileges of community and shared a strong sense of responsibility towards others and the future. New Orleans, and the "Madagarday" (Mardi Gras day) festivities must have offered him an eye-opening view of the world.

> On Marde Gras day, everybody is masked and going round the street heaving flour at everyone they meet which is a pity as it is 15 dollars a bbl!
>
> I would give all my old boots if I was at home for this city is the worst place that ever was made yet—nothing but fighting all the time.
>
> I shall not be able to bring much tin with me. I like a fool spent two dollars to a boarding house. I had to buy a belt and knife. I expect that I shall have to buy a pair of sea boots and a suit of oil clothes. I don't spend no money for nothing foolish, I have not been to the theatre since I have been here. And somebody has been so good as to steal my two postage stamps that Mother gave me.

IN HIS LETTER DATED FEBRUARY 24, 1855, SOLON DESCRIBED LIFE IN NEW ORLEANS, INCLUDING MARDI GRAS DAY CELEBRATIONS.

To My Mother

New Orleans Sat eve 24, 1855

Dear Father I received your kind letter by the hand of Capt Chase for I went on board the bark the next day after I wrote to Mother the captain is going to give me Ordinary's wages out of this port we have discharged three days I don't know wheather we shall go to N. Y. or Baltimore but I expect the latter all the crew have come back the cook left last Wednesday and he has had a tearing spree but is coming back the day after tomorrow we shipped a cook the day after the Hey left and the captain drove him ashore the next day.

The captain has used me first rate the whole voyage but he is very hard on the man at the whell Sam has come back he shipped to go to Liverpool in the seaking he stayed on board one day and was so lonesome he had to come back.

I shall not be able to bring much tin with me I like a fool spent two dollars to a boarding house I had to buy a belt and Knife and I expect that I shall have to buy a pair of sea boots and a suit of oil clothes I don't spend no money for nothing foolish I have not been to the theatre since I have been here and somebody has been so good as to steal my two postage stamps that Mother gave me.

If we go to Baltimore you can tell what time I shall be at home better that I can myself if we go to N. Y. I shall be at home by the middle of april. I don't know of any thing more to tell you So I shall drop a line to Mother

Dear Mother

well marm I have got here and I do bless god for you and me both and as I got your letter this afternoon I shall take the opperchance to answer it this evening so brother hill has raised hell generally I am glad abby has got convArted that is about as goo a thing as could be done, and I suppose that Charles Wardwell will get so pious he will give away both his horsus to Sasah and Charles have got convarted very goo thing the old spouter has not got Jed, France, or Lucius warmed I am cock sure that Lushe is not I suppose the sewing circle is gone to pot since father hill has come. poor sam has just been having a puke what you might call a rum shit from between his teeth he has been sober all the week but he went up to night and come down roaring drunk I expect he feels good about this time.

It is a very good thing for the dog that thare is no snow for I suppose that Ame has him in the harness every time there is a chance.

I tell you what we had some rather blue times on the passage out we had the worst squall in the gulf that ever I heard tell of I and frank chase was at the lee easing reefing the mainsail and she rolled so as to touce his feet in the water I have heard of vessel's sioling their yard arms in the water but that was coming the nearest that ever I want to see it this is the wetist craft that ever I was in and the fastist sailer.

you may expect me home as soon as I can get thare cleverly I suppose that I must say a word to L. J. so Goodby answer this Dear Mother from your own boy Solon

Dear Sister Lucy

As you gave me a sample of your penmanship I suppose I must give you a little of mine this has been a busy week in this city their has been two holiday Madagarday I think they call it and washington's Birthday Madagarday every body is masked and going round the street heaving flour at everyone they meet which is a pity as it is 15 dollars a bbl the captain has used me very well but gives sam fiddlers change the second mate is a regular tobacco mill always with a tear on the end of his nose like a trailing rat I was his second choice we washed our figurehead and cutwater off in the first blow that we had I want you to give my love to all the girls and boys and keep them stra [illegible]. tell amy that I shall write some to him the next time Direct your letters to the care of J. P. Whitney saying Please forward you see I have wrote a goo long letter so good bye my love to all

from your brother Solon Hanson

THE WHARF.—GAUGING OIL.

IN HIS LETTER DATED MARCH 17, 1855, SOLON WRITES THAT THE SHIP IS LOADED AND BOUND FOR NEW YORK.

New Orleans Sat March 17, 1855

Dear Mother we are all loaded and bound for New York she is deep as she can swim you may expect me home by the middle of April I am well but have been very sick while we loaded up the coast Sam, Littlefield is very sick and is going to the hospital the crew have all left but I and Hiram Closson both mates have gone two I write this in great haste for I have but a few minutes I intend if I have the good luck to get to N York alive to come home by steam boat [illegible] *caso write me in N York I have had no letters since the one dated the 12 Feb we shall take steam for the balize this afternoon Give my love to Father Lucy Jane and Amy and keep as much as you want for yourself tell Sally Gray I was much obliged for the Valentine*

> *Your own boy Solon Hanson*
> *S N H*

Overall, Solon's first major voyage was a success. His next challenge was the perilous fishing on the Grand Banks. Here, the weather patterns are bitter cold and unforgiving. After such a diverse and sometimes hostile crew on the bark, the conditions on the Grand Banks were comparatively friendly.

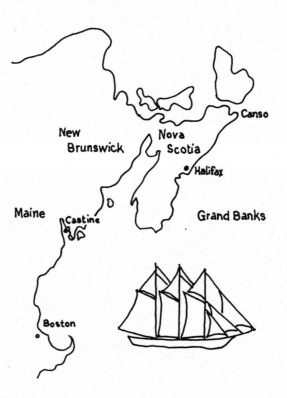

New
Brunswick

Nova
Scotia

Canso

• Halifax

Maine

Castine

Grand Banks

Boston

Chapter 9

1857 GRAND BANKS FISHING

THE GRAND BANKS OFF NEWFOUNDLAND were productive and popular fishing regions in the 1800s. The Grand Banks is located in the North Atlantic Ocean southwest of Newfoundland, Canada. This region is comprised of several shallow banks that rise from the continental shelf, and are approximately 560 km (about 350 miles) in length, with depths ranging from 37 to 183 m (121 to 600 feet). Lieutenant Charles Wilkes first surveyed the George's Shoal, the Bank, and the fishing ground east of Cape Cod. In 1837, the United States Depot of Charts and Instruments published the charts of the Wilkes survey. They became invaluable navigation resources for fishermen.

Where the cold Labrador currents and the warm Gulf Stream cross there are shallows and slopes rich with plankton, resulting in an abundance of Atlantic cod, haddock, pollock, and hake. Cod tend to be bottom-dwellers, swimming near the sea floor. Spring time and spawning time they reside near the bottom of shallow water. In winter they seek deeper water.

Cod

The weather patterns provide many bitter cold storms and heavy fog, which, coupled with the shoals, make navigation difficult and dangerous. O'Leary's dissertation, "Maine Sea Fisheries: The Rise and Fall of a Native Industry 1830–1890," describes many of the events. Between 1830 and 1867, Castine lost fourteen vessels and 51 men in these waters. Castine lost the *Rich* on the Grand Banks in 1867, although no lives were lost. The following year, Penobscot lost the *Ocean Wave* and nine of her crew on the Grand Banks. The acceptance of danger was ingrained into the life of New England communities. According to O'Leary, in 1886, the United States Fish Commission reported that "probably no other industry carried on in this country shows yearly such a loss of life and property as the New England fisheries."

Fishermen feared the combination of a Northeast gale and a snowstorm. The shoal ran north-south and west. To avoid wrecking on a lee shore, eastward was the only exit in rough weather. Snow could limit visibility to half a vessel's length during daytime and to nothing at night. The crewmembers could scarcely see each other and often could not see the lookout man or hear him above the wind. A vessel could encounter another vessel in the same dire position before either could take corrective measures. Even if other vessels became aware of such a situation, often there was no room to maneuver to rescue anyone. Lives and ships were lost.

Despite the dangers, the call to go to sea was unquenchable. By the 1850s, captains competed for the best berths on the Banks. The competition led to physical entanglements and sabotage. One way to make it difficult for other vessels to fish was to spread something foul in the water so folks downstream were affected. The refuse from cleaning fish (called gurry or fishing offal) and fish oil were often dumped into the water. Too much gurry fouled the water and the fish would leave. Sabotage sometimes included breaking portions of a competing vessel or their fishing equipment.

From their common bonds and need for protective alliances, comradeship arose on the crowded Grand Banks. Solon reported interactions with many other schooners from local fisheries, including the *Albion*, the *John Perkins*, the *Alciope*, the *Mentora*, the *Orient*, the *Olio*, the *Sarah & Pulia*, the *Marietta*, the *Old Rick* and the *Glendower*. Solon looked for, but did not find, the *Sun*, a ship that his father fished aboard. Records of the *Albion*, the *Mentora*, and the *Glendower* document that these schooners had departed from Castine and fished on the Grand Banks until September or November. With similar itineraries and being neighbors at home and at sea, the vast majority of the Down East fishermen seemed to work together instead of against each other. Vessels homeward bound carried letters to family and friends from other vessels.

Solon's letter home expressed his joy in sailing with a crew of Down

East fishermen, having a successful and productive haul, making some money, and seeing other vessels in the area. His letter underscores the popularity of the region, with his sightings of 30 vessels. In the 1820s, Maine produced about one-fifth of the tonnage of fish in the United States and had half of the fisheries. By 1860, Maine was second in the nation, with annual fishing revenues of over one million dollars.

Solon's letters are an excellent record of the rate at which the fish were caught. Judging by his report of the haul that other vessels made, these figure seem to be typical of vessels that sailed the Grand Banks in the 1850s.

The cod fish were cleaned, dressed, and partially salted down to preserve them. According to O'Leary, the purchase of salt for use on the fishing voyage accounted for approximately one third of the cost of outfitting the Grand Banks schooners. The origin of the fishing bounty lies in the compensation for import duties on fishing salt used for fish that were exported from the United States. Back at port, the cod were washed and re-salted for drying or pickling; the re-salting process required one pound of salt for every two pounds of cured cod.

Not all fish would be exported; some were consumed at home. Salted-down cod would keep through the winter. Undoubtedly, Solon and his family enjoyed regular fish meals. Fish chowder was a family favorite. Recipes have been passed down through the generations. The two great-granddaughters of Solon's sister, Lucy Jane, recorded the recipes provided here.

Fishing changed a lot in the decades that followed Solon's expedition. In *Abigail and Sarah Hawes of Castine: Navigators and Educators*, Mark Honey describes some of the innovations. In 1858, the *American Eagle* of Southport revolutionized the fishing industry by doubling the rate of catch. The *American Eagle* carried a number of small dories on board. The fishermen were paired off to man the dories, returning with a full load of fish. This was successful and quickly became the standard method of fishing. Edwin Solon Conner, grandson of Lucy Jane Hanson E. Peterson, went on such fishing excursions. Family stories from him relay the added dangers he faced. Quite often a dory pair would become lost in zero-visibility fog and have to navigate based on the sounds sent out from other teams or the crew on the vessel. If they became lost and unable to follow sound, they would retreat, rowing west in hopes of finding shore and rescue as the fog lifted. There were times when retreat was not possible. This meant disaster for the dory.

Cod was considered an important food source. In the South, the cod went to feed plantation slaves in the decades before the Civil War. Fish were a major United States export, enabling the developing nation to import luxury items and goods it could not produce yet. Congress encouraged the cod industry. The first Congress in 1789 held the protection of the cod fisheries as one of the primary considerations. In part, this interest arose because President Washington was extremely fond of cod fish and every Saturday night, he ate a dish of boiled potatoes, beets, and onions with "soaked-out" cod fish all covered with fried pork scraps and egg sauce. Congress raised fishing bounties throughout the years until shortly after the Civil War. The national interest in subsidizing fisheries had many facets beyond presidential cuisine. The Navy benefited from the technological advances of sailing vessels, especially in the era following the War of 1812. Steamships made sailing vessels less attractive for the Navy after 1860.

Following the Civil War, in 1866, Congress removed the bounty placed on cod. The Maine fishing industry suffered severe economic losses. Only half of the cod fisheries remained after five years with no bounties. The fishing industry was thrown into turmoil and many fisheries were bankrupted due to the removal of these bounties and by the Morrill Act of 1861, which placed a stiff tariff on salt. The fishing was extremely hazardous and better jobs became available. Financially, Castine, Maine never recovered from the losses due to the decline in the fishing industry.

O'Leary's dissertation proposes that the fishing industry would have been successful even without the bounty, and that the bounty imposed an economic democracy by allowing the working class to be part owner of the vessel and catch. Many historians argue that the removal of the bounties and the loss of fishermen to the Civil War impacted the industry. O'Leary counters that the loss of fishermen was insignificant compared to the number of apathetic fishermen who prolonged their voyages to avoid confrontation and tended to be a little older than a typical soldier in the Civil War. O'Leary proposes that the industry declined for a number of complex and interrelated reasons, including wartime inflation which doubled the cost of outfitting for a fishing voyage; exploitation by insurance agencies in the aftermath of several accounts of privateering; technology advances using fishing nets which required a greater outlay of capital and provided a greater return; declines in food costs of competing products; disruption of trade with New Orleans; increased import duties and required materials; and other causes, coupled with the untimely repeal of the bounty. The era that followed was one of monopoly and centralization fueled by a technology revolution that streamlined the fishing industries and complementary industries.

Solon's letters seem to support O'Leary's interpretation of the significance of the repeal of the bounty law. His descriptions of life at sea and the hardships that were faced securing business suggest that the industry would have declined with or without the bounty during the latter half of the century. The California Gold Rush and other opportunities inland promised adventure and fortune.

Needless to say, the persons who had benefited the most from these bounties were hit the hardest. These included whole families from the under-educated, working class. O'Leary's dissertation further emphasizes how crewmen were victimized by the fishing industry's trickle-down debt.

O'Leary's research included the demise of the *Glendower* mentioned in Solon's last letter. This spotlights one meaning of the term "owing your soul to the company store." The crews were seldom paid before the catch had been processed and marketed by the fishing industry, vessel owners or merchants, which could take a good part of the year. This meant that their expenses in the meantime had to be carried on the company's books, usually with interest added, until payday. In the *Glendower* case, the crew arrived home August of 1858 but were not paid until the following March, just before they shipped again. The cycle of debt could be impossible to escape.

Solon's mention of being "payed off" as soon as they cleaned up at port was the exception and not the rule. Solon briefly visited home and then signed on as crew of a cod-trading vessel headed for New Orleans.

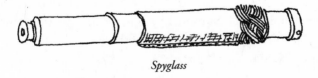

Spyglass

IN HIS LETTER DATED JULY 5, 1857, SOLON REPORTS THAT THEY ARRIVED
AT THE GRAND BANKS ON JUNE 10 AND BY JULY 17 THEY HAVE CAUGHT
OVER 20,000 FISH. ADDRESSED TO CAPT. JOHN HANSON, PENOBSCOT
MAINE. DELIVERED BY "POLITENESS OF MR. ORDINAY."

Sunday, Grand Banks. Eastern Shoals

July 5, 1857

Dear Father

*We arrived on the bank after a prosperous passage of six days without reefing
or taking in a sail. we had a small blow the 2 day of June and a very heavy
one the 10 we rode until we parted our chain it blowed for about four hours
a regular hurricane. we was very lucky about finding the shoals there was
four of us got here the same day we had the pick out of them and took the
one the rattlesnake laid on last year it is a long narrow shoal but the fish are
very large there is now about 30 sail on here now and there is some gouging
for a berth. We have got our jibboom rigged in and our spare anchors lashed
on the rail and are all ready to try titles with any of them we have been here
about 23 days and [illegible] of that time have swing off 8 days we have
got 15,000 rousing fish. The Albion Capt Thompson the John Perkins and
Captain Brewster all lay here in company with us.*

*Capt Lucy will be ready to sail for home in about ten days I shall send it
home by him.*

*I dont know of any news in particular to tell you. Gus is just what I
took him to be he's just the same all the time and Saih is the laziest devil
that ever was little Rube is a very good cook and sends his love to [illegible]
de. Eben Teakettle turns out to be a real smart boy and catches a good share
of fish Sam Patten is a first rate man. he and I heave together I shall wait
until Brewster get ready to sail before i finish this. Friday 17 as i have a
chance to write a few lines I might as well improve the time we have now
twenty thousand and upwards Capt Wardwell in the Alciope is here with us
he has about 30 thousand and all the scrall line there is on the bank his crew
stole a lot down to the southward and the other day a brig run her scrall
under his stearn and in the morning he was minus about 1,800 fathoms he
come alongside of him in his boat but he did not get but very little satisfaction. he got under way and come down bye us and shook a piece of line at us
and flourished knives and clubs. he thought twas us.*

we invited him to come aboard if he thought it would be wholesome for him. if he spoke english he must have been highly flattered with what we said to him so he swore sacre and went off. we see the Mentora the 9th with 14 thousand I saw Lide and pete but I did not have a chance to go aboard Conley says lide is a first rate boy.

Sunday 19 Capt. Brewster will be ready tomorrow so I will put on the finishing touches to this Epistle: *We finish the week with 22,000 we might have had ten more if the vessels to the Southward of us had not gurried up our shoal. I am in hopes we shall be ready to start by the 25th of August tell Ame to take Good care of that Colt and keep all the girls civil till I and Rueben gets back. Give my love to Mother, Lucy Jane, Granny. Ame. Hermy. and all the Girls I shall be glad when we leave this barren country*

I remain the same old child Sode

IN HIS LETTER DATED AUGUST 10, 1857, SOLON REPORTED THAT THEY HAVE CAUGHT AN ESTIMATED 33,000 FISH.

Grand Bank August 10, 1857

Dear Mother

as I have a chance to send a line by the smilax I thought you might like to hear from me we have 33,000 fish

18. Barrels of oil 12 Barrels of bait and 45 Thds of salt if nothing happens to us we shall be ready to start by the 1 September if we could only lay on our shoal we should have all the fish we wanted in ten days. there is more fish here than there is any where else on the banks the vessels on the rocks are doing nothing. on the rocks or on the body of the bank there is no fish at all.

we celebrated my birthday by getting twelve hundred fish of which I got about three hundred of I have better luck this year fishing then I ever had before high line every night I have not seen a sick minute since I have been gone. and we have got the most amiable crew that ever was in the world we have plenty to eat and drink and little Rube to cook for us and are in all good health and spirits you may look for us by the 10 of Sept Give my love to all the boys and girls I shall write a line or two more if I have a chance

Affectionately Yours
Sode

**IN HIS LETTER DATED AUGUST 12, 1857, SOLON REPORTS THAT THEY HAVE
CAUGHT ALMOST 35,000 FISH.**

Wednesday 12

*To day it blows a heavy gale from the SSW which swings us off our
shoal. we have now almost 35,000. if I had taken that third Gus offered me
I should have made about forty dollars a month but if I had taken it we
should not have got half sea fare I suppose but twenty eight dollars is not
bad pay for a boy.*

*Jim Thompson in the albion has got over 40,000 large fish he will be
ready for home in a short time. Rufe Leach and Bob in the Sarah & pulia
had only 13,000 a week ago last sunday. they have done the slimmest of any
vessels on the shoals. The Marietta had 30.000 the first of this month and
the Glendower 18,000 they both went to the southward about a week ago.
the old rick is on here leaking twelve thousand strokes every four hours.
Dave Sawyer in the magnet had to go home on account of his crew staving
up his water. I have not seen sun or heard of any Castine vessels lately but
these. I suppose the old alciope has been at home sometime she had a good
pile of fish and plenty of scrall line of all the devils to steal from frenchmen
the Dunbars and Leaches beat them all I shant be at all sorry when we get
home and washed out for I have got about as much of these banks as I want
this time If nothing happens we shall be paid off as soon as we get washed
out and I can take up that note from pel which will save a little nitres.*

*Give my regards to all inquiring fiends meems in particular Rueben also
disires to be remembered to all*

> *your loving son*
> *Sode Hanson*

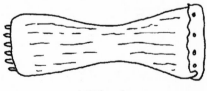

Fish scaler

Fish Chowder Family Recipe
> (from the kitchen of Marian Helen Conner Myers)

2 lbs. of halibut or haddock	1 teaspoon salt
2 cups water	freshly ground black pepper
2 oz. salt pork (diced and fried)	1 quart milk or canned milk
2 onions sliced	2 tablespoons butter
4 large potatoes, diced	

1. Simmer fish in water 15 minutes. Drain and reserve the broth. Flake fish and discard bones and skin.
2. Cook pork in heavy skillet until crisp and golden.
3. Simmer onions in pan with water until tender. Drain.
4. Simmer potatoes in another pot of water until done. Drain.
5. To the fish broth, add enough water to equal 3 cups. Then add fish, potatoes, and onions. Bring mixture to simmer.
6. Add milk. Heat to serving temperature.
7. Ladle into bowls and sprinkle top with the diced golden pork and if desired you may add a little of the pork grease.

Fish Chowder Family Recipe
> (from the kitchen of Virginia Conner Moseley)

2 lb boned, skinned halibut or haddock cut into 1 ½ inch chunks
1 ½ cup fresh corn kernels cut from cob
2 cups heavy cream and 2 cups milk
1 ½ Tablespoons flour
1 ½ Tablespoons butter
2 teaspoons chopped parsley
1 cup diced salt pork or 1/2 lb. bacon cut in squares
¾ cup finely chopped onions
3 medium potatoes, peeled and diced
1 ½ cup water
1 ½ teaspoon salt
½ teaspoon freshly ground black pepper
1 teaspoon dill weed

In a large, heavy kettle, sauté salt pork until it is crisp and fat has been rendered out. Remove bits and reserve for garnish. (Do the same if bacon is used.)

Add onion to fat and sauté until tender (pour off some of the fat if there is a lot). Add potatoes, water, salt and pepper. Bring to a boil, cover and simmer 12 minutes.

Add dill and fish and simmer covered for five minutes. Fish will appear not quite cooked. Add corn and cook two minutes. Pour in cream and milk. Bring mixture to just below boil.

Blend flour and butter together and whisk into the soup heating long enough to slightly thicken it, but keeping it barely simmering. Sprinkle the parsley and add reserved pork or bacon bits (good with or without the corn).

New Orleans

New York: D. Appleton & Co.

Chapter 10

HURRICANE IN NEW ORLEANS

FTER THE FISHING SEASON, the fishermen returned to other jobs like farming or sailing on trading vessels. During the decade between 1848 and 1858, Castine's exports to the Gulf Coast included cod, mackerel, other fish, hay, ice, granite, and paving stones. Fish was the predominant product. Shipments were usually made in November and December after the fish had been processed for market.

In the 1850s, Castine was the wealthiest of all Maine fishing ports on a per capita basis. This was achieved to a large extent by its eight fishing companies and the fact that fishing was the major occupation. Local investors and operators of the fisheries owned most of Castine's vessels. Shipments on the Castine vessels were often joint ventures working with agents in New Orleans.

During this time, Castine's shipyards built square-riggers for New Orleans investors. The major shareowners and registry were in New Orleans. These included the *Picayune*, the *Castine*, and the *J. P. Whitney*. Samuel Noyes built the *Picayune* in 1857. The owners were Samuel, Samuel T., and Joshua Noyes of Castine and R. B. Sumner of New Orleans. The *Picayune* was 172.2 feet long, 35 feet wide, had a depth of 17.5 feet and was 974 tons.

Solon took a position aboard the *Picayune* working for Captain John Brooks who was the ship's master. The *Picayune* left the port of Castine in November 1857 with a cargo of 200 drums of cod, 250 barrels of mackerel, and 120 tons of hay. Following a twelve-day journey from Castine, the crew of the *Picayune* arrived at their first destination with ease. With the exception of the cook, the crew of Down East fishermen was an easier group to work with compared to a typical crew. For Solon, this experience was better than his last venture to New Orleans.

> We arrived after a safe and prosperous passage of twelve days from Castine we was two days towing up from the bar to the city we had a fresh blow from NW the day after we sailed and run under close reefed topsails for 36 hours and for all our crew was nothing but downeast fishermen we handled the ship as if she was a pilot boat the mate says he never saw a better crew for his life.
>
> I was third man picked when we chose watches the second choice of the Mates.

Captain Brooks was a sober man, and Solon's cheerful personality was a contrast to his solemn nature. Solon struggled with several social, work and weather problems throughout his stay in New Orleans. He considered leaving the *Picayune* for various reasons. Captain Brooks was having difficulty securing business for their next trade voyage. The pay was low compared to other opportunities. He disliked waiting at the port because he detested New Orleans. Finally, the prospect of promotion was small because Captain Brooks thought a sailor needed many years of experience before becoming a mate. Solon's ambitions were clear:

> Our ship has not got a freight yet, but they think she will have one soon. The times are hard as ever; the wages are only 15 dollars an month and a great many ships are hauling up. . . . I shall strive to make a sailor of myself as fast as I can, but I think my chance's for promotion will not be so good here as they would in some ships. Old Brooks thinks that a man ought to go to sea twenty years before he is competent to go second mate. He don't believe in boy officers.

There was a lot of work to do while they waited for their next voyage. The majority of the minor repair work on shipboard was done by the sailors themselves. Solon provided details of the maintenance he and the crew performed aboard the *Picayune*:

> I think we can finish up by next Saturday the ship looks like a fiddle everything has been painted scraped and

slushed form keel to truck and now they have got a lot
of holystone and prayer books and we have to get down
on our knees and rub rub rub all day long my knees
have got so hard that I have a strong notion joining the
Methodist church.

Time in port kept everyone busy on maintenance and repairs. Decks
needed to be swabbed and sanded, rails and trim needed sanding, and
there was tarring, painting, and polishing. Sanding the deck entailed the
process of 1) wetting down the deck (rain helped) 2) covering the surface
with beach sand 3) rolling the "holystone" across the deck 4) sanding the
smaller areas with "Prayer Books" 5) washing the sand off the smooth surface 6) drying the fresh surface with rags. The holystone is a huge soft rock
that was rolled across the surface of the deck by hauling it on ropes. The
prayer books were smaller soft rocks that worked liked sanding blocks.
The rails and trim were sanded with pieces of canvas and sand. The process
of maintaining the woodwork was tedious and strenuous. The finished
ship was a work of art in which the entire crew took great pride.

*Solon Hanson
and his friend*

IN HIS LETTER DATED DECEMBER 13, 1857 TO HIS MOTHER IN PENOBSCOT,
SOLON DESCRIBES HIS TWELVE-DAY VOYAGE FROM CASTINE TO NEW
ORLEANS. (NOTE: A STEVEDORE IS A PERSON IN CHARGE OF LOADING AND
DISCHARGING CARGO.)

New Orleans La Dec 13/57

My Dear Mother

*We arrived after a safe and prosperous passage of twelve days from Castine
we was two days towing up from the bar to the city we had a fresh blow
from the NW the day after we sailed and run under close reefed topsails
for 36 hours and for all our crew was nothing but downeast fisherman we
handled the ship as if she was a pilot boat the mate says he never saw a better crew for his life. I was the third man picked when we chose watches the
second choise of the Mates. The Officers are good beyond all my expectations
the ship is first rate two she does not leak a drop. all thanks to george Bridges
say I and all the rest cry* amen.

*I have not received any letters from home yet but it is hardly time yet.
Capt Gray has been gone from home about a fortnight bound to Liverpool
his family knocked off keeping house about a week after he left and are
now boarding at a stevedores about two miles out back in the city our two
mates have gone out to see them and I set out to go . . . with them but I was
afraid the old lady would be after me with a tomahawk and I thought if she
caught me she might distress me the worst kind.*

*I expect we shall all have to leave the ship the times are so hard the
castine has been hauled up here most of five weeks Capt Brooks says he shall
keep us by the ship fifteen or twenty days and then if we dont get a freight he
will have to discharge us but he will hate to discharge us bad enough. he has
not spoke a cross word except to a couple of boys who let a topgallant stunsail
boom fall from the upper maintopsail yard and it fell on deck and broke in
three pieces and then fell overboard the old person was rather put out everything he has said to me is* how do you head my son *or something like that
and the mate is one of the best fellows you ever saw all the boarding house
runners was mad as the devil because we would not go with them they swore
we was fishermen every bugger of us if we have to leave we can go on board
a ship called corinthian bound to trieste the captain is an old grey bearded
fellow he has took great shine to us he says we are* shust de poys he vants

Write soon dear Mother I shall expect a letter by next sunday

Give my love to all
I shall write every chance
Give my love to all
your own boy   S J Hanson

IN HIS LETTER DATED DECMBER 17, 1857 TO HIS SISTER, LUCY JANE, SOLON
DESCRIBES LIFE ON THE PICAYUNE AT PORT IN NEW ORLEANS.

New Orleans Dec [illegible] *17/57*

Dear Sis

Having a few moments of spare time I thought I would take me pen into
my toes the way the kennebec folks do to let you know how we are getting
along. well first and foremost five of the boys have left Jo Dunbar Side Ed
John Perkins and Sewall Pruden they have gone on board a bark bound to
Boston so you will probably see them again before long.

We have got most all dischared I think we can finish up by next Sater-
day the ship looks like a fiddle everything has painted scraped and slushed
form keel to truck and now they have got a lot of holystone and prayer books
and we have to get down on our knees and rub rub rub all the day long my
knees have got so hard that I have a strong notion of joining the Methodist
church.

The chances look slim for our getting a freight if we don't get one in a
week from next saterday we shall all have to be discharged and I shall have
the blessed priviledge of going ashore to a sailor boarding house which is very
pleasant and that you may peace

Mr Ozro Frithy is ashore here with his advance all worked up he is in
rather a hard corner for a green boy to be placed in. and Bill Bridges is here
to be his joinry second mate of a Havre packet and will sail in a few days
his health is good but I rather think his funds *are rather small. If I have to*
go ashore I shall get a ship bound to Liverpool or Havre for if I should come
home this next spring. I should have about as much money as I did when I
went with Chase and I am not able to make such expensive voyages as that
was.

The Mate opened his heart the other day and bought us a bitch pup it was covered in fleas and had the summer complaint the worst kind and the perfumery that rose from the little beast was a caution to the nasal organs of all concerned so this morning Charley Hatch give her a pass over the side.

Tell Ame that it was a good thing for him that he staid at home this winter for the ships are all hauling up the times are dreadful hard there is more men ashore here than ever their was before all the boarding houses are swarming.

I have not seen any thing of Capt Grays folks yet but some of the boys saw them the other day coming from the post office they was dressed up to the nines Charley Foster and I are going to hunt them up next Sunday I expect they feel so big that they will hardly speak to me (but a mans a man for a Hat)

SOLON CONTINUED HIS LETTER THE NEXT DAY.

Friday 18

I am about half sick to day. we lay the third tier from the wharf and have to hoist it all by hand and it was almost draged us out.

I have a good mind to go steamboating out here for this or rather on this rolling muddy the wages @ 65 dollars a month.

The Mate has just handed me a letter from you and I have devoured its contents very greedily. I am very sorry for that dear old person and think she might to have old frio to comfort her a little Give my love to all the boys and girls. tell Lude not to make herself uneasy I should think she would know better than to take any notice of them row breedind old devils. I am going to write to her next Sunday remember me to Mr. Renter and all inquiring friends.

I remain S J Hanson
PS I wrote to mother last Sunday I want you to write every chance S J H

IN HIS LETTER DATED DECEMBER 21, 1857, SOLON WRITES ABOUT OTHER CASTINE SAILORS IN NEW ORLEANS AND ABOUT WAITING FOR COTTON FREIGHT TO COME DOWN THE MISSISSIPPI RIVER.

New Orleans Monday 21/57

Dear Father

I received Lucy Jane's letter dated the 6th of this month of which I made

mention of in the litter which I was writing at that time. to her there is
nothing new at present our ship is not got a freight yet but they think she
will have one soon the times are hard as ever wages are only 15 dollars an
month and a great many ships are hauling up

Capt Simpson's ship the castine has commenced loading with cotton she
is bound to Cork for orders.

Bill Linton who married Lucy Wescott is here second mate of the ship
Corinthian of Portland bound to Hull and from there to Boston

Remember me kindly to all. take good care of that colt and the oxen and
tell Ame to break them steers so they will be handy by the time I get home
again

I shall strive to make a sailor of myself as fast a I can but I think my
chance's for promotion will not be so good here as they would in some ships.
old Brooks thinks that a man ought to go to sea twenty years before he is
competent to go second mate he dont believe in boy officers

The Bark that those boys went in left here the 19th. I expect they will
come right home they might as well for they want good for anything except
Jo Dunbar. the mate picked Silas out. just as you said he would for an old
garden toad and Edwin was all jaw like a sheep's head.

Reuben bids fair to become a right likely hand and Eb Connor is a first
rate man.

Sunday 27 I have not had a chance to finish this epistle till today we
spent a very merry Christmas and John Diamond honored the day by giving
Tom a licking and getting drunk

Mr. Sumner paid us a visit on Christmas. he told the Capt to keep us
all just as long as we wanted to stay so I suppose we shall all stay by I dont
know anything new to tell you of we have got no freight yet. the river rises
all the time there is now about 7. knots current in the river and the cotton
comes down pretty fast and the prospect is that the times will soon be better

I have had only one letter from home yet and have wrote three and the
one I got was chock full of (said ashout) let me have an answer as soon as
you get this. My love to all

Solon J Hanson

In Solon's letter of December 17, 1857, he uses the phrase "But a mans
a man for a hat" which was a quote or an allegorical reference to "But
a man's a man for all that" from a book that belonged to his sister: *The*

Poetical Works of Robert Burns, Phillips, Sampson, and Company, Boston, 1856. Inside her copy, someone has written that the book was presented to Lucy J. Hanson by Noah Mead.

Honest Poverty

Is there for honest poverty,
    That hangs his head, and a' that?
The coward slave we pass him be,
    We dare be poor for a' that!
For a' that, and a' that,
    Our toil's obscure, and a' that,
The rank is but the guinea's stamp,
    The man's the gowd for a' that.

What tho' on hamely fare we dine,
    Wear hoddin gray, and a' that?
Gie fools their silks, and knaves their wine
    A man's a man for a' that;
For a' that, and a' that,
    Their tinsel show and a' that:
The honest man, tho e'er sae poor,
    Is king o' men for a' that.

Ye see yon birkie, ca'd a lord,
    Wha struts, and stares, and a' that
Tho' hundreds worship at his word,
    He's but a coof for a' that,
For a' that, and a' that,
    His ribbon, star, and a' that
The man of independent mind,
    He looks and laughs at a' that.

A prince can mak a belted knight,
    A marquis, duke, and a' that;
But an honest man's aboon his might;
    Guid faith, he mauna fa' that!
For a' that, and a' that,

Their dignities and a' that,
The pith o' sense and pride o' worth,
Are higher ranks than a' that.

Then let us pray that come it may,
As come it will for a' that,
That sense and worth o'er a' the earth,
May bear the gree, and a' that
For a' that, and a' that,
Its coming yet, for a' that,
That man to man, the warld o'er
Shall brothers be for a' that.

Notes in *The Pocket Book of Verse* edited by M. E. Speare, Collector's Edition Pocket Books, Inc. New York 1940:

Gowd means gold
Hoddin gray means homespun
Birkie means young chap
Coof means fool
Aboon means above
Mauna fa' means claim
Gree means have the first place

IN HIS LETTER DATED JANUARY 12, 1858, SOLON REPORTED THAT THE ADAMS HAD ARRIVED, AND THAT HE HAD PICTURES TAKEN. THE WORD 'FIZOG' IS A YORKSHIRE COLLOQUIALISM FOR 'FACE.' THE REFERENCES TO 'PIC' ARE THE SHIP *PICAYUNE*.

New Orleans Jan 12 1858

dear sis

The old Adams arrived here last Saterday after a passage of 20 days not quite so quick as ours she lost a man fourth day out his name was William Andrews he married some kind of a Butler Steele *over on gray's ridge the boys have all left her. I got that letter from John Pete the night she got in I also received the one you wrote the 27 of Dec. and the one dated the 31 very glad indeed to have so many letters I am as well posted up in penobscot news as if I was there myself you tell Elisha and Pete that I wish them much joy and*

Neims also there is eleven of us still by the pic *and I guess that they will keep us the boys that come out in the old Adams dont seem to like their watch and watch boat you know that they would not come in the pic because Mr. Wescott was so ugly their mate Cole Mead has worn out a pair of* Bran new boots kicking *them* asses

I expect that father has got back from Boston by this time the next time you write tell me if he has got that money from Gus yet I am very anxious to know John Pete and I went up and got our fizog's *taken together last sunday Johns is taken first rate but mine looks like the devil*

I dont think I shall favor you with anymore of my pretty penmanship so good bye/your Bub

Sode

**IN HIS LETTER DATED JANUARY 1858, SOLON WRITES TO HIS BROTHER
AMOS ABOUT LIFE AT THE PORT. HE WRITES THAT ONE OF THE CREW WAS**

Solon with an unidentified friend, possibly John Pete

**RECOUNTING A FAMILIAR LEGEND ABOUT A ROCK-HEAVING GHOST IN
BROOKSVILLE, WHICH IS NEAR CASTINE AND PENOBSCOT.**

Dear Ame

As you and Granny are the only ones I have slighted among our folks I suppose now is the time to make up for it. I like the ship first rate as well as the Officers & crew we have been here over five weeks and have got the ship fixed

up in fine style I expect if we have to stop here till spring we shall go to Russia John Pete has not shipped yet but he expects to go on to N York in a bark

I suppose that Ed Lide and Joe have got home by this time they have been gone from here a month and over so look out for your tail or he Ed will have it sheared smack smooth he said he could afford to stay at home one winter for by Gard *he had one hundred sixty dollars laid up there that is forty dollars less then his marm let Calvin have to go to the golden regeions with. I have stolen time to write this letter out of my nooning tonight I will finish it it is now 10 Oclock and the boys have all turned in except Henry who is relating a legend and a very marvelous one to of Brooksville it is nothing more nor less than that rock heaving ghost story. John Pete has just gone from here he has shiped in that Bark bound to york with five more of the crew of the old Adams they will sail in a week I dont know of anything more to say except to give my love to all. Your loving Brother Solon J Hanson*

P.S. Direct your letters to the same old place J P Whitney & CO if I go to Liverpool they will send them there

Now I am going to give you an Issaac Leach flourish this is a boblink

I want you to let me know if Keith is married Amos W. Hanson

tell Lucy Jane that I shall send my ambrotype home before I sail John P will sail next week for N. York Rueben sends his love to all our folks and Granny in particular on account of that harb tea *story*

Sode

Storms at sea and in harbor often caused damages that the crew had to repair. On January 16, 1858, New Orleans was ravaged by a hurricane that resulted in losses of $500,000 worth to shipping. Various reports regard the storm as a tornado, gale, breeze, or hurricane. *The New York Times* reported that the storm lasted half an hour; other accounts say it was only five minutes. The *New Orleans Picayune* printed:

> The sudden and furious gale of yesterday afternoon, more particularly described elsewhere, has, we regret to learn, proved very severe upon both the steamboats and shipping in our port almost every interest, indeed, exposed thereto on the river. The amount of damage we are, as yet, unable even approximately to estimate. It must, however, be very great; but that is nothing compared with the loss of so many valuable lives. The following are the particulars, condensed and classified so far was we have been able to obtain them. We will simply provide, however, for the better understanding of the reader, that the gale proceeded from a southwesterly direction, and was but of about five minutes duration. It was, in fact, a hurricane.

Solon described the extensive damage:

> Last Friday, we had a regular hurricane. It is the worst one that there ever was in New Orleans. It broke 45 ships from their piers. The Ocean Monarch of New York and the Golden Eagle of Kennebuck, both of them about 22 hundred tons, parted their moorings and came down on a large Rockland ship and two New Orleans ships and they came down on the Castine. Picayune and a large English ship and the lord knows how many more, broke away after that we went down about three miles below the city and brought up stearn in the mud bank over on the Algiers side. Although we was in the thickest of the fight, we got out of the scrape the best of any of them. We had our monkey sail rooted off by a Bath ship, and we also lost our jibboom, big bowen, anchor,

split stern, and rudder; and scrubbed off a good lot of molding on the stern.

Under the headline "Great Hurricane in New Orleans," the January 20, 1858 *Weekly Courier* of Natchez, Mississippi, printed that the damages were in part due to disrepair of the wharves:

> Great injury was also done to the shipping lying along the Levee, involving in many instances loss of live. A great portion of the damage done may be attributed to the wretched condition of the wharves in the third and fourth districts. It is hoped that the city authorities of the Crescent City, will endeavor to remedy such, evils in the future by an appropriation of city funds sufficient to keep the wharves in good repair.

Solon wrote about the loss of life:

> The ship rattler of Boston had a couple of men blown off her main topsail-yard. One of them was the second mate and the other the captain's son. The latter fell between two ships and was jammed all to bits. The second mate struck . . . the main hatch head first and drove his head into his body so nothing but just his hair could be seen of it.

His eyewitness account is validated by the damage to the first and second districts reported in the *Courier*:

> In the First district we learn that the second mate of the ship *Rattler*, at post No. 23, John Anderson, a Swede, was blown from aloft, fell upon the decks, and was instantly killed. The son of Capt. Forrester, acting as the third mate of the *Rattler*, was blown overboard and drowned.
>
> The ships *Stateswan*, *Alice Counce*, and *Spark of the Ocean* lying at No. 32, were blown adrift and compelled to anchor in the stream. The ship *Mont Blanc*, lying at the same tier, was also somewhat damaged.

Three men were capsized in a skiff, opposite No. 27, and drowned. Their names or further particulars could not be ascertained.

In the Second District the ships *Plus Ultra*, *Joseph Rowen*, and the barks *Prince of Wales* and *Jacob Prentiss*, were blown from their moorings and drifted down the river. Some of them received considerable damage, having come in collison wiht the barks *Evelin* and *Alberta*, the bowsprits of both of which were carried away. They finally came to anchor, however, below the Point.

During the gale, and before these vessels had parted their moorings, a man who was standing on the gangway of one was blown overboard and was drowned. His name could not be ascertained.

Solon's letters related the activities aboard the *Castine*, another New Orleans owned square-rigger launched in 1857 from a Castine, Maine shipyard. On December 13, Solon wrote that "times are so hard the *Castine* has been hauled up here most of five weeks." On December 21, Solon wrote that "Captain Simpson's ship, the *Castine*, had commenced loading with cotton she is bound to Cork for orders." Following the January 16 hurricane, Solon wrote about damages sustained by the *Castine*:

> The Castine is all stove to pieces. Seven thousand dollars won't make as good a ship of her as she was last Friday morning . . . There was three ship's with anchors all in a mess with ours and the Castine's. Our crew went on board the Castine and broke her patents right off.

Solon relayed Captain Brooks' solemn personality, but also showed the Captain's appreciation for a humorous situation:

> The Captain he is the most sober old child you ever saw. I have not seen him laugh as Gus say but twice since we have been gone. When we was clearing our anchors, They had a man over the bows of the Castine in a bowline and nine of her longshore men could not haul him in. I advised them to take him to the capstern and then a very hard smile come over his mug.

By "capstern" Solon means they should use a capstan, a large vertical axis drumhead by which anchors were hoisted and heavy equipment was handled, implying the man overboard was rather heavy. Unfortunately, the damages sustained by the third and fourth districts were anything but humorous. The *Courier* reported:

> In the Third District the ships *Ocean Monarch* and *Golden Eagle*, lying at post No. 42; ships *Nuremberg Gottenberg* and *Forest Eagle*, lying at No. 43; ships *Castine*, *Peperell*, *Picayune* and *Tchernaya*, at No. 45; ships *Ann Washburn*, *Houghton* and *Ellen Stewart*, at No. 46; ships *N. Larrabee*, *W. V. Moses* and *R. D. Sheppard* at No. 47; ships *C. C. Duncan* and *Rochester*, at No. 48; and ship Arthur, at No. 49, were all blown from their moorings, wharves, and sustained more or less damage. They drifted down the river and finally came to anchor below the Point. The *Ann Washburn* lost her bowsprit and sprung her foremast.
>
> The towboat *Anglo-American*, rounding to with a ship in tow had her chimney blown down. Other ships, in this gale, were blown adrift, suffering material damage thereby.
>
> In the Fourth District, the ships *Sultan* and *Charles Pennell*, at No. 53; *Wesser*, *Elvire Owen*, and *Kittie Floyd*, at No. 54; and *Julius* at No. 61, were all blown across the river, and are now at anchor near the opposite shore.
>
> The ship *Zenobia* carried away a portion of the wharf at No. 54, and about fifty bales of cotton went overboard from her.
>
> The *Charles Pennel* is considerably damaged; the *John G. Caster* and *Forest King* materially so, by collisions.
>
> The amount of loss sustained by ship owners and other's interested, must necessarily be very great; but as yet, the amount cannot be definitely ascertained. The gale was of very short duration but of unusual severity.

The damages to the *Castine* were repaired and it continued operation. On January 30, 1858, Solon wrote that the *Castine* had freight for

St. Petersburg and would be ready in about three or four weeks. February 9, he wrote that he expected they would go to Russia as they had just secured freight. On February 26, about the same time that the *Picayune* was ready to go, he wrote that the *Castine* was ready for sea.

Solon explained the bleak nature of their business waiting to secure a profitable freight over the Christmas holiday. In previous years, it would have been more common for a 19-year-old to be promoted to mate, and it was probably still common on smaller vessels. Now with the popularity of sailing and fishing, this was one of the predominant occupations in Maine at a time of increasing competition from other trade transportation. Solon found himself in a lower-paying job with no growth potential for years to come. In recent past years, he would have found himself in a job with rapid growth potential in one of the most lucrative industries of the Industrial Revolution. The storm in New Orleans added to the pre-Civil War economic woes. Yet, Solon had accepted a position of second mate with Captain Gray; work that would start after Solon returned from a nine-month voyage on the *Picayune* with Captain Brooks.

Records of outward manifests of various Castine vessels are kept in the National Archives, records of the Bureau of Customs (Record Group 36), Collection of District Records, District Coastwise Manifests. Around the same time as the voyages of the *Picayune* and the *Castine*, the *Adams* departed from Castine on December 18, 1857 with a cargo for the Withlerle and Company firm of 110 drums of dried cod and 46 half-barrels or kegs of cod tongues and sounds and with cargo for fish-merchant Samuel Adams of 120 barrels and 174 kegs of mackerel. Samuel Adams was the managing owner of the *Adams*, and was one of the owners of a Castine fish company and a leading Castine merchant who could afford to finance more than six of the largest Grand Banks schooners, such as the *Mary Brewer*. The shipment was cosigned to Robeson, Dennett and Company, and a New Orleans firm.

The departure date is consistent with Solon's following report of seeing the *Adams* in port. Solon wrote that old *Adams* arrived in New Orleans on Saturday, January 9, 1858, after a passage of 20 days. On the fourth day out, one of the crew, William Andrews, had died. Solon wrote of the crew: "The boys that come out in the old *Adams* don't seem to like their watch and watch boat . . . They would not come on the *Picayune* because

Mr. Wescott was so ugly . . . Their mate Cole Mead has worn out a pair of Bran new boots kicking them asses." Solon wrote that some of the crew were shipping out of New Orleans aboard a different bark. On February 9, Solon wrote that the *Adams* would be ready to ship to Trieste in three weeks. On February 26, he followed up that the *Adams* was ready for sea.

IN HIS LETTER DATED JANUARY 17, 1858, SOLON WRITES ABOUT ABOUT THE HURRICANE OF JANUARY 1858 THAT DEVASTATED NEW ORLEANS.

New Orleans Sun eve Jan 17/58
Dear Father

We have just got cleared up from a little the worst sunday's job it has ever been my lot to have.

Last friday we had a regular hurrycane it is the worst one that there ever was in new Orleans it broke 45 ships from their piers. the Ocean Monarch of N York and the Golden Eagle of Kennebunk both of them about 22 hundred tons parted their moorings and came down on a large rockland ship and two N Orleans ships and they down on the Castine. Picayune and a large English ship and the lord *nose how many more broke away after that we went down about three miles below the city and brought up stearn in the mud bank over on the algiers side although we was in the thickest of the fight we got out of the scrape the best of any of them we had our monkey sail rooted off by a bath ship and we also lost our jibboom big bowen anchor split stem and rudder and scrubed off a good lot of the moulding on the stearn. the Castine is all stove to pieces seven thousand dollars wont make as good a ship of her as she was last friday morning*

The ship rattler of boston had a couple of men blowed off her main topsailyard one of them was the second mate and the other the captains son, the latter fell betwen two ships and was jammed all to bits the second mate struck on the comings on the main hatch head first and drove his head in to his body so that nothing but just his hair could be seen of it there was also a lot of pieces ships broke from & the upper I believe about fifty but the wind blowed then across the river one of them took a wharf with her with sixty bales of cotton on it

the theatre folks have just come down about blued up so I will postpone this till tomorrow night

Monday 18.

I guess I shall have a chance to finish tonight if they dont wake up. we got back to our berth last night and very glad of it we had a hard one to clear the anchors there was three ships anchors all in a mess with ours and the castine our crew went on board the Castine and broke her patents right off the damage done to all shipping is estimated at about $500.000 which is quite a pile of earthly possessions. five hundred dollars will cover all our damage but I suppose you have got tired of this. I will get the paper that has got all the particulars and send it home to you.

we have first rate times here in the ships we have not got a freight yet although we have been laying over six weeks it is a devil of a drill though I assure you I had rather be at sea by a long chalk but I expect I might look a good deal farther before I should find a better ship I guess I shall stay by her for the voyage if nothing new turnes up but the fact is I am getting too ambitious. I have got sick of stopping forward and eating hoss *I want to get aft a little farther if it is in the* Cabin water Closet *The captains wife is the best little woman the* lord *ever made she will talk to any of us right before the Captain he is the most sober old child you ever saw I have not seen him laff as Gus says but twice since we have been gone when we was clearing our anchors they had a man over the bows of the Castine in a bowline and nine of her longshore men could not haul him in and I advised them to take him to the capstern and then a very hard smile come over his mug. write every chance you give my love to all I shall let you know just as soon as we get a charter*

your affectionate son Solon J Hanson

tell Lucy Jane if she dont write to me soon that I shall be mad give my love to every one no matter whither they want it or not.

Solon's letters attest to the trials and tribulations of waiting for the opportunity to make the next voyage. Records of Castine trading voyages illustrate the trade patterns that took place. Some followed the New Orleans-Liverpool-Castine triangle. Others made runs from New Orleans to Boston to transport cotton to the New England textile mills. The triangle trade arrangements exported cotton and other goods to Europe and Russia. Many vessels stopped at Cadiz, Spain, for salt on the voyage home.

These voyages were lucrative and gave Castine economic independence. The southern fisheries needed the importation of cod and mackerel from Maine. This brought Maine into being part of the cotton trade and international trading. Missing from all the documentation of this are the operating conditions the captains and crew faced. The personal letters and diaries of the sailors reveal hidden costs of this business which include the lapse time when sailors were discharged due to lack of business. The costs of hardships on the crew become difficult to enumerate. Even with the consistent bounties at the top level, Solon's words describe a system that is eroding at the bottom.

William Hutchinson Rowe wrote in his book *The Maritime History of Maine*, that:

> Cargoes were hard to secure, freights were low, and the demand for new ships had begun to decline rapidly. Even in the peak year of 1855 Maine built vessels sold for twenty-five per cent less than twelve months previous. Since 1853 the apprehensive had feared and warned of approaching commercial disaster. In the Fall of 1857 the storm broke in full fury. For the next eight years there faced the shipping interests of the country first the ravages of a severe economic depression and then—civil war. These conditions earmarked and coincided with, but did not cause, the decline of the American merchant marine. In short, depression and the toll on shipping taken by the Confederate raiders merely hastened the complicated process of the ultimate substitution of steam for sail.

Solon's three-month stay at the port in New Orleans underscores the problem. Despite the hardships they endured, the *Picayune* was finally loaded with cotton for a voyage to Russia. Solon continued on the *Picayune*.

IN HIS LETTER DATED JANUARY 30, TO HIS BROTHER AMOS, SOLON WRITES ABOUT THEIR WORKING CONDITIONS AND THAT HE HAS SENT

"AMBROTYPES" HOME. AN AMBROTYPE IS A PHOTOGRAPH CREATED BY IMAGING A NEGATIVE ON GLASS BACKED BY A DARK SURFACE.

New Orleans Jan. 30. 1858

My Dear Brother Ame

It has been almost three weeks since I have heard from home and I have almost got discouraged I suppose you and Father have got home long before this time and I should have thought you might have written to me before this time if you dont write soon I shall begin to get pretty cussed *mad. everything is as dull as ever we have got to lay here the lord only knows how long before we get a freight we have got our damages about all repaired that we received during the very heavy gale of the 16th of this month I tell you what Ame if you had been here then you would have seen something to stick your eyes out at more than you will if you should live on that old farm a thousand years. the way the bowsprits got ripped up and the big sticks come tumbling down was a sin to Davy Crocket the Castine has got a freight for St Petersburg she will be ready in about three or four weeks I dont know but what I shall I leave this ship yet she is a regular floating poor house the usage is good but the grub as aunt* Anna *said of her boys.* Oh God *that old nigger of ours is not worthy of a seat in hell he will soak beef in water that has been drawed a week and if we growl to him about it he will break out into something like this* who de deb'l you tink goin to draw water for darn sailors by gorra ise gut miff to do tend to de cabin grub *the more we threten to thin out his hair the uglier he gets the other morning there was some mackerel I come into the forecastle that stunk enough to knock down our old sow so we all swore (old shell like) that we would not turn too on such* damed *grub so when the second mate come to call us (as none of the rest would speak) I had to stand spokesman I told him that I should not do a stroke of work until I had some breakfast he made considerable noise but did not frighten me but very little he went aft and told the mate and then he come forward as noisy as young thunder he said he had worked without any breakfast before now and those who could not work on that grub might go ashore "so Reube. Henry. John Conner. Maid Dunbar and I packed up our things without delay and was on the* pint *of leaving when the mate come forward as clever as a pig he promised us all the good fashions you could think of he said we should have just as good grub as there was in any ship in New Orleans and everything he could think of besides to keep us by I told him that we was not curs when we said a thing we meant it. he was*

*so clever that we concluded to go to work again but Frank Wardwell and
Eb Connor acted like regular mean stinks they went right out and went to
work. but us five did not get any breakfast but then we got a little satisfaction which as jerry Pint says done* equally *as well I have found Capt Grays
folks and they are as kind as can be Capt Gray has been gone from liverpool
37 days bound to New Orleans so we expect him here very soon I guess I
shall go with him if I can get a chance I can get a second mates berth on
board of a prospect bark and I am almost good mind to take up with the
offer.*

*John Pete sailed last Tuesday with seven more of the boys that come out
in the Adams they will probably be at home in three weeks I sent an ambrotype home to Mother by Jerry Dunbar and one for Lude by John Pete I have
no more news to tell the boys are all well and in good spirits Hen Stover
sends his love to you and all the rest of our folks I have not had a letter from
home for three weeks except one from Joe Dunbar an that was about that
story of the hugging scrape I shall send you a copy of it when I write again
answer this as soon as you get it*

Your loving Sode

*Tell Ross not to be discouraged for Hen Stover says when he comes home
he shall* marry her up *give my love to the old dear also to Aunt Ruth, and
uncle vess Lude Taylor and Sally and dont forget to talk dotian to neems*

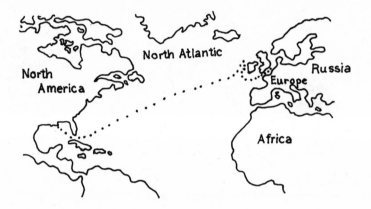

Chapter 11

TO ST. PETERSBURG

SOLON'S ACCOUNT OF THEIR DRAMA-FILLED MONTH in New Orleans recounts life-threatening natural disasters, the daily violence and obscenity along the waterfront. A nighttime fire burned up six steamboats, which drifted ablaze among the shipping boats, burning the sides off of two ships and a schooner. The *Picayune* narrowly escaped damage when one of the blazing steamboats came perilously close.

When the steward of the *Picayune* was tried for shooting at the cook, Solon was summoned as a witness. At the court, he saw "the animals that was brought out of the lock up; it was morning after the masquerade day the women dressed in men's clothes and the men in women's, all put in for getting drunk!"

Being the seaport of the Mississippi River, New Orleans was the meeting ground of Americans, Native Americans, English, French, Cubans, Russians, and others. The clashing ethnic backgrounds gave rise to violent disagreements and contests for dominance in the cultural hierarchy. Free African-Americans struggled for identity on the eve of the Civil War. Yet they were accepted by the Northerners and found reasonable work at the docks and in sailing. Solon's reference to the cook as "old nigger" was probably not as derogatory and racist then as it would be now. But the Down East boys had a rivalry with Frenchmen flamed by the recent wars and fueled by competition for fishing and trade rights. The Frenchmen and New Englanders could exchange heated words with a gale force stronger than a November hurricane.

With the future dependent on uncertain crop yields, catastrophic weather, fishing intake, trade agreements, and possible war, the city never slept. In his letters home, Solon conveyed images of death:

> Somebody gets killed every day so we can have some-
> thing to talk about. There was an Indian murdered by
> three Englishmen. They found him laying on some cot-
> ton they were watching, and stoned him to death. They
> will be hung and it serves them well.

The long delay in New Orleans was costly and the crew became anxious to get underway. Desperate for low-cost labor, the crew of the *Picayune* shanghai a Frenchman. Shanghai, or "white slavery," was the practice of kidnapping a person for compulsory service aboard a ship. A person could be "recruited" to the crew by dragging him on board, usually accomplished by getting him drunk and disoriented. The person "fell asleep" on board while the ship was in port. Before he awakened, the ship departed. Once at sea, the person had no choice but to work. From about 1850 to 1940, Portland, Oregon, was notorious for shanghaiing people and used a network of underground tunnels to imprison and move them. Apparently, though, Portland was not the only United States port in which this practice took place.

In March 1858, the *Picayune* departed New Orleans with a cargo of 3,667 bales of cotton and a destination of St. Petersburg, Russia. The crew of the *Picayune* faced a number of sailing challenges on their voyage to St. Petersburg. During the passage across the Atlantic Ocean, Solon could not correspond with his family, but he purchased a diary and maintained daily records.

In contrast to the chaos of port life, sailing the Atlantic proceeded with clockwork precision. A strict schedule had to be maintained to ensure the functionality of the ship and the safety of the crew. The woodwork, sails, and ropes required routine inspection and repair as they were exposed constantly the battering of waves and wind. Solon's diary illustrates the skill needed to manage a transatlantic voyage. Seamen had to sail with whatever the wind presented and work it with the ocean currents. Solon appears alert to the changes of the wind and the sails needed in differing conditions, despite the illness he had since leaving New Orleans. He was looking forward to becoming Captain Gray's second mate when he returned.

On April 10, 1858, Solon discovered that the Frenchman had died. Solon writes:

> We had a man die on the passage, one we shipped in New Orleans, a Frenchman. They shoved him aboard after getting him drunk and took his advance. He had only been out of the hospital three days. He died without anyone's knowing it. I came in the night to ask him how he was and he was stiff as a post, so I and Frank Wardwell had the honor of sewing him up.

Solon's diary reads:

> Saturday April 10, 1858 found a man dead in his berth after a sickness of three days' hove the ship too and consigned him to the deep (The dead reign there alone)

After 52 days at sea, when the *Picayune* reached the Straits of Dover, Solon sent home another letter dated May 14. In reference to the anticipated birthing event of the Captain's wife, Solon writes, "I hope I shall be invited to the groaning." Apparently, a birthing event provided significant diversion.

IN HIS LETTER DATED FEBRUARY 9, 1858, SOLON DESCRIBES A FIGHT IN WHICH THE COOK AND THE STEWARD TRIED TO KILL EACH OTHER. SOLON MENTIONS SENDING HOME "TO POT RATS," HIS DOWN EAST PHONETIC FOR "TWO PORTRAITS."

New Orleans Feb Tues 9 1858

Dear Father

I received your letter last Tuesday and today a first *one from Mother and Lucy Jane and very glad to hear that you are getting along so finely I also got a letter from Ike Leach and it was chock full of* turnover's *he is well and at the same old business he say's he is coming home in the spring we have lots of fighting and jawing Maid Dunbar has left and the Capt refused to pay him he sued and got the case wages and everything to go with it he is bound to N York in the Brig Fanny O Fields and Cad is going mate of her*

The cook and steward have quarreled the whole voyage and last sunday the cook tried to cut the stewards throat with a razor and the steward fired a pistol at him the ball just cleared him and that's all his face was all covered with powder he went up town to complain of him and not having any pass a policeman lugged my young man *off they then come down and took the steward and kept him in the* Chokey *one night so Rube had to take charge of the skillet they all like his cooking first rate. Eb Connor is sick with the slow Fever and is pretty well down to heel the rest of the boys are all well and in good spirits they are the most sober steady set of boys it has ever been my lot to fall in with the Old Adams has taken up for Trieste and will be ready in three weeks. the bark that John Pete was in sailed a fortnight ago today for N York and has probably arrived before this time I sent home to* pot rats *by him I suppose he will go right home after he gets there. I suppose you feel quite tickled about that line* twixt *you and Uncle Ned we have not got a freight yet although we have waited long enough* God nose *we expect to go to Russia I am bound to stick by her let her go where she will I expect if we go to Russia that the second mate will leave and go home if he does I hope Frank Wardwell will take his place but I expect the Capt will gets some* dago *but I am quite sure Wescott will have me in his watch he has his ups and downs Just like the rest of us but take him all round is a pretty good man the Capt is the same old sixpence he never says anything but what is to some purpose. I have wrote all this in my nooning so you see we have good times I will finish tonight and mail it tomorrow. Well evening has come and with it a gift from the steward in the shape of a sperm candle so I take the carpenters room and fire up our damages are all repaired that we received when we were adrift they expect Capt Gray here very soon he has been out nearly forty days from Liverpool bound here. there is some talk about our cotton's coming down next Friday but I dont know whether it is so or not I should like to have been at Whithums serenade first rate I expect Amos had quite a time that night. has Silas blowed any about his* vige *in the Pic all the boy's here call him the old helmsman Oh . . . by the way I have had a letter from Joe Dunbar since he has got home it was the foolishist thing you ever saw it was about what Ad told Cal he said that* Aderson *told Calvin that he was sorry that every body was down on our folks and (that was what Aderson said) you tell sis and Ame to get that circulated for a bye word but not let any body know where they got it from he ended by telling me that Lude was my* sincer lovur *and that was the jist of the subject for*

which favor I was most d_____ly obliged to him I have got a valentine for
my dear old ant *it is a two faced woman the face she carries behind folks*
backs looks very much like the old dear I wish Ame much Joy give my love to
Ada. I am sorry for poor Ephe and hope he will save his arm. I wrote about
a fortnight ago to Ame and sent you a weekly paper about the same time
hope you have got both write often it is a great treat to have a letter from
home give my love to all I shall always remain the same old Sode Hanson

**DATED FEBRURY 22, 1858, THIS LETTER FROM SOLON, IN NEW ORLEANS, TO
HIS FATHER IN PENOBSCOT, MAINE, DESCRIBES WHAT HAPPENED WHILE
THE SHIP WAS BEING LOADED FOR A VOYAGE TO ST. PETERSBURG, RUSSIA.
THIS INCLUDED BEING SUMMONED TO APPEAR BEFORE COURT FOR A TRIAL
ABOUT THE FIGHT BETWEEN THE COOK AND THE STEWARD.**

New Orleans Feb 22, 1858

Dear Father

I received your letter dated 10th feb yesterday. very glad to hear from home
indeed! we commenced loading a week ago today for St Petersburgh and
shall be ready for sea in a month at farthest. Rueben is telling a story about
Daniel leach getting hove out of a wagon and bothers me so I cant think
of much to say. he has been cooking a spell and turns out a d_____d sight
worse than the old nigger! the steward has beem tried for shooting at the old
cook it was thrown out of court I was summoned as a witness but was dis-
charged without giving in my story it was good as a poor play to see the ani-
mals that was brought out of the lock up it was morning after the masquer-
ade day the women were dressed in men's clothes and the men in women's all
put in for getting drunk! the ship E. D. Peters is here bound to liverpool and
wants a crew I guess John Pete is sorry he did not stay out here and go in her
she wants a set of down east boys! bad! and a third mate John Pete could get
the berth in a minute if he was here the mate speaks very highly of him

   we got the same old fodder that we have had all the time. famine stares
us in the face every where we look it is a pleasant thing to go to Russia and
have to discharge cargo on what we get to eat. I should like to call in to
Lucy's kibberd *to night and see what there was stowed away there I dont*
think I should refuse to eat my supper to spite my marm. Capt Grey has
arrived at the bar but has not towed up yet he has had a very long passage!

the old Adams is nearly ready for sea. we had a very heavy fire here sat,y night among the steamboats on the Algiers side. burning up six of them three boats burnt off their fasts and came over among the shipping burning the sides off of two ships and a schooner one of them came close to us but we received no damage from them! the guns are banging away now and have been all day celebrating the birth of Washington (and if you plage him you will get a cussed infurnal licking) *things go on just about the same somebody gets killed every day so we can have something to talk about there was an Indian murdered by three englishmen they found him laying on some cotton they were watching and stoned him to death they will be hung and* sarve em well right *Henry Stover sends his respects to all he is a real good fellow although he does give the truth some dreadful stretches in some of his Brooks'ille yarns Eb Connor will be out of the hospital in a week. he is getting better real fast he had a pretty hard time of it! Charley Foster will go the voyage I expect! Cad Dunbar has not gone yet we are having about as much of a winter as you are I guess we have cold wet rainy weather two or three days and the sun will come out hot enough to roast the devil for a day or two just for a change we have several pets on board the ship and all there* shitting apperatus *are in excelent repair we have a rooster that crows all night long and a screeching pup five doves and an old hen things that we could not do without on any account! Feb 26 I have not been able to write for the last three days so I will begin now. Gray has arrived and he has the Sea Bell. I have been twice up to see Bill. George was gone both times they are both in good health. I received three letters from home yesterday and very glad was I I have not had any before for three weeks tell Amos I think he has taken quite a literary turn I have got two* missiles *from him. if you keep on you will have quite a stock of cattle. I shall send you home money to paint the house next fall and if I can I will send it before I leave here! the freights are rising and times are getting a little livlier the bark that Ed & Side went home in has come here again she brought our anchors to supply the place of those we lost in the squall. the Castine and Adams are ready for sea. Eb Connor will come out of the hospital tomorrow he has got real smart. John Connor is mad as the devil about what Emily Palmer said about him she said he promised not to give the crook of his elbow to any girl while he was gone he swears he never will go home again as long as he lives.*

　　March 3rd I have been waiting for Eb Connor to get out of the hospital before I sent this he come over to day and looks thin as a hatchet we shall sail the 15th of this month so it will be useless for you to write after you receive this. you may write the first of may. direct to me, ship Picayune ___ Cronstadt care of American Consul. we shall go from Cronstradt to liverpool or bristol. then to New York or Boston. be gone about nine months Grey has arrived all right *I shall go with him next voyage and second mate in the bargain dont say anything about this away from home H Saunders is going greys mate next voyage my love to our folks ____*

     Always the same Sode J Hanson

DATED MARCH 19, 1858, THIS LETTER FROM SOLON, IN NEW ORLEANS, TO HIS FATHER IN PENOBSCOT, MAINE, PROVIDED SOLON'S ITINERARY TO HIS FAMILY AS THEY WERE ABOUT TO DEPART FOR ST. PETERSBURG WITH 3,667 BALES OF COTTON.

    New Orleans Mar 19 1858

Dear Father

We are all ready for sea and shall go down river tomorrow Carries 3,667 bales.

    I have been sick with summer complaint for a week but am some better now. write to me the first of May. direct to me ship. Cronstradt care of American Consul. shall be back to york in Dec. next guess I shall come down and have a look at you then. give my love to all.

    I remain the same
    Solon J Hanson
PS Bill and George W __ are going to Boston

    S. H

SOLON'S POCKET DIARY FOR 1858.

On the first page he wrote the following:
    Solon Hanson
      Castine
      John Hanson
    Hancock County Maine

Ship Picayune
Mr. J. B. Desisle
   Lamoine Me.
care of J. Machelle & Co.
   Old Lavee Street 129
   on board Schr Eastern Queen

On the next page:
   Portland
      Maine
   care Sargent & Lord
      Schr Fred Dunbar

Pocket Diary for 1858

3/12   bought this book and commenced keeping a diary
3/13   hauled ahead and let ship Forest Eagle out and took inside
       berth. cotton coming all the time Henry and Frank are watch-
       ing tonight
3/14   washed decks and got three dollars of the Capt paid J. Conner
       $1.50 and squared up this is fourteen sundays we have laid
       here and I hope it will the last
Got a letter from Mother.
3/15   Fresh breezes from SE and clear in fore noon hereto fore and
       main top gallent sail upper and lower [. . .] topsail. sick
       with flying axehandles
Tuesday
3/16   Finished hanging sails sick enough today up but still cralling
       round.
3/17   still sick but about got a dose from mate but did not do me
       any good at work lashing spars getting ready for sea. sent
       down royal yards
3/18   Charley Devereux come aboard scraped all the bright spars.
       laid up part of forenoon—got a letter from home
3/19   finished lashing spars and hatch houses. work on sennet.
       Crew had liberty in afternoon. four staid on board.
3/20   filled water and lashed side skids finished loading crew come

on board towed down someone stole a lot of cloths from our ship but none of mine.

3/21   arrived at the bar towed outside
       anchored rigged out jibboom and set up gear cleared up decks.

3/22   washed decks and set up head gear in afternoon sent down mizzen top gallent yard and mast and lashed them Winds SSE and foggy.

3/23   Got underweigh from the bar wind NW and haxy afternoon chose watches I am in the Mate's watch and was coming out to N Orleans at ten P. M. calm and rainy haauled up main-sail ends rainy.

3/24   Begins Moderate with rain at six PM light winds from N by E and cloudy at ten smart breeze from NNE and clear steering SE middle part of light breezes & cloudy latter part calm with very heavy showers. thunder an lightning.

3/25   begins with very heavy rain and calm latter part light breeze from SE and clear End calm and rainy

3/26   commences with light breezes and clear middle part light and rainy at half past three wind come in squall from North ends heavy gales from N ship under lower top sails foretop mast staysail

3/27   Rather more moderate middle part calm with heavy swell latter part moderate breezes from NE and clear at 8 PM tacked ship—

3/28   Commences with fine breezes from NE and clear at six PM saw the light on the Moro at twelve tacked ship

3/29   Commenced with fine breezes from NNE and clear weather passed cutter in sight of Moro off Havanna at 12 Tacked ship at 6 PM fished cross jack and caught a dolphin

3/30   begins with fine breezes from ENE and clear washed fore-castle out in forenoon—latter part fresh breezes from E by N handedfore and main top gallant

3/31   Commences with fresh breezes from SSE and clear at twelve set fore and Main top gallant sails ends freash gales and clear heavy head sea still had very heavy squalls from SW with rain close reef top sails.

4/1   Begins with very heavy gales from SSW at 6 AM more moderate set upper top sails and courses fore and main top gallant sails ends very heavy squalls from SW with rain ship under lower topsails foretop mast staysail

4/2 Commences with heavy squalls from SW to W and severe rain set top gallant sail at 12 furled them and Mainsail at 6 PM ship under close reef topsails foresail foretopmast stayssail heavy sea running

4/3 begins with fresh breezes from WSW and rainy Middle part more moderate set topg'tsails K coneses ends fresh gales from NNW ship under lower top sails and courses steering NE

4/4 First part of this day fresh gales from NNW and clear weather latter part fine breezes and pleasant saw several breezes steering NE

4/5 begins with light breezes from NNW and continues moderate throughout saw a number of dolphins but did not have the luck to catch any.

4/6 Commences with light winds from SW and pleasant at ten AM had a smart squall from NE at 12 a wind hauled to SSE ends fine breezes and clear

4/7 begins with light breezes from NNE and clear latter part clear and Moderate wind NEE. SE and very smooth seas.

4/8 Commences with light breezes from ENE and smooth sea Cook struck Bob over the mouth with a dipper and cut his lips bad ends very light breezes and smooth. set up head gear.

4/9 Begins with light breezes from SE and pleasant at 10 AM spoke ship

A [illegible] -lgerine from Shanghai bound to New York one hundred days out. ends fresh gales from SW and clear steering NE by E.

4/10 Fresh breezes from SW and clear at 3 AM found a man dead three days was a Frenchman hailed from Paris shipped in New Orleans aged 35 years. name unknown. buried him at 9 AM after heaving the ship too.

4/11 All this days smart breeze from SW. WSW and W and pleasant weather ends with wind WNW light breezes and rainy steering NE by E.

4/12 Begins with fresh breezes from NNW and cloudy Middle part light breezes from N by W and hazy latter part calm

4/13   *Commences with light breezes from SSE and cloudy middle part smart breezes from S and clear latter part smart gales from SSW ends clear steering NE by E*

4/14   *Begins with heavy gales from SW and clear. weather at 4 PM took in topmast and lower lower steen [illegible] ends with fresh breezes and cloudy heavy sea running steering NE by E*

4/15   *Commences with very heavy gales from SW with frequent and heavy showers and squally ends with wind W by N heavy gales ship under lower fore and main topsails foresail steering E*

4/16   *Commences with very heavy gales from*
        W by N and clear weather and cold enough to freeze the old boy at 12 [illegible] more moderate Meade sail ends moderate winds cold and cloudy.

4/17   *Begins with fresh breezes from WSW and clear still very cold middle and latter part winds light and variable have had a very bad pain in my right eye this last day of two*

4/18   *This day begins with fresh gales from SSE with snow and rain at ten wind hauled to W by S smart gales and clear ends heavy gales and clear weather*

4/19   *Commences with fresh breezes from NW and clear very cold latter part wind N . . fresh gales reefed topsails took in topgallent sails ends clear and cold*

4/20   *Begins with fresh breezes from NW and clear weather—latter part heavy gales reefed topsails handed topgallent sails ends heavy gails hail and snow*

4/21   *Commences with fresh breezes from WNW and clear latter part calm*

4/22   *Begins with moderate breezes from NE and cloudy Middle and latter part heavy gales and rain squalls ends very heavy gales from NE ship laying too under close reef main topsails*

4/23   *Commences with fresh gales from NE and clear middle part moderate made sail saw a ship to windward with main top gallant mast gone ends fresh gales from SSE reef topsail [illegible] and rainy*

4/24   *Begins with fresh gales from South with thick weather Middle part smart gales from SSW and clear ends fresh breezes and cloudy*

4/25   Commences with fresh breezes and cloudy wind SW by S
        middle part light breezes from SSW and foggy latter part calm

4/26   Begins calm and thick fog heavy swell from SE Middle and
        latter part moderate breezes from NNE and clear weather
        and quite warm for the latitude we are in 53° 30'

4/27   Commences with fresh from NNE and clear weather ends
        clear wind NNE throughout

4/28   Begins with moderate breeze from N by E and cloudy latter
        part fresh breezes from WSW and rainy ends heavy squalls
        from NW with frequent showers.

4/29   Commences with fresh wind from NNE round to NW and
        squally ends heavy gales. ship under lower topsails fore top-
        mast stay sail hail and snow

4/30   All this day very heavy gales from NNE and very squally with
        snow rain and hail at 8 PM wore about within miles of the
        north of Ireland blowed mizzen stay sail away ship under
        lower [illegible] spain topsail drifting SSW

5/1   Begins with heavy gales from NNE at 5 AM parted weather
        main top sail sheet furled the sail at noon set lower fore top-
        sail reef foresail steering SW ends very heavy gales and bad
        sea running

5/2   Commences more moderate set lower main top sail

5/30   Rec'd 5 Rubles of Capt Brooks ship
        Picaynne =$4—

6/6   Rec'd 3. Rubles of Capt. Brooks $4—

6/13   Recd 5 Rubles of Capt. Brooks $4—

6/27   Recd 5 Rubles of Capt. Brooks ship Picaynne

7/4   [an erased entry dealing with money again]

[under Memoranda in back of diary]

1857 November 16th shipped and went on board ship Picaynne
       bound to New Orleans for 14 a month. Sailed the 24th arrived
       the 11th December—Commenced loading with cotton for Russia
       Feb 18th, 1858 Sailed for Russia the 21st of March 1858
       Saturday April 10, 1858 found a man dead in his berth after a
       sickness of three days' hove the ship too and consigned him to
       the deep (The dead reign there alone)

Arrived in Cronstadt
May 24

DATED MAY 12, 1858, THIS LETTER FROM SOLON, IN THE STRAITS OF
DOVER, TO HIS FATHER IN PENOBSCOT, MAINE, PROVIDED SOLON'S
ITINERARY TO HIS FAMILY AS THEY CONTINUED TO ST. PETERSBURG.

Straits of Dover May 12, 58

Dear Father we have arrived so far on our voyage safe and sound. we
have been fifty two days from New Orleans tried to go to the Northward
of Scotland but had such heavy weather we had to keep away and go up
through the English channel. had rather a rough time on the NW coast of
Ireland came very near getting jammed in Donegal bay we had a man die
on the passage one we shipped in NEW Orleans a frenchman they shoved
him aboard after getting him drunk and took his advance he had only been
out of the hospital three days he died without anyone's knowing it I came in
in the night to ask him how he was and he was stiff as a post so I and Frank
Wardwell had the honor of sewing him up. I get along first rate with both
officers and crew we shipped most all dutchmen they turn out to be a real
civil crowd I am in the mates watch again and picked out to steer in heavy
weather Reuben has not steered but two tricks since we left Castine he is
rather a plain old tar Eb Conner is well and eats more than old Josh Bridges
the boys are all well and Henry is a kind of boatswain the Capt's. wife is
incient *and* spex fine sune *I hope I shall be invited to the groaning we*
shall get to Cronstradt in about 15 days with a common chance the ship is
crank as the devil *she has come across on her side all the way. we have been*
in the Channel 12 days with a head wind all the time so you can bet there
has been some brace pulling we took a dover pilot last night he will take us
up in the North sea clear of everything before he leaves Capt Brooks likes the
down east boys better then old shells he says they steer better tricks and are
better men anyhow. the ship still continues tight as a cup and behaved her-
self like a lady up in the bad weather I want you to send word to all the boys
folks when you get this and let them know that they are in good health. we
shall be back to some part of the United States by the last of Sept the mate
says she will go to York or Boston but I guess New Orleans will be as likely
to pick her up as any other place I guess I shall go one voyage more before I
go home there is nothing so very funny about it after all. we get the same old

*grub ring stoppers and shank paniter but still I manage to keep fat as ever
there is more danger of getting the scurvy then the gout. we have got a fighting man for a cook he struck an old swede with a long handled dipper that
give him a mark on the lip that he will carry with him as long as he lives
but he takes very good care not to hit any of our crowd as Hermy says he
knows* dam *well what he'd get but he is a first rate cook for all that if it was
not for him we should all starve to death he is very good to me. and leaves
something for me to eat in the galley most every night I suppose you have
gone to farming to a dead ruin this spring I suppose the stock is growing up
finely. there is nothing like the old farm after all to take comfort on I should
like to step in and take a look at you all a little while but cant do it just yet
tell Lucy Jane I want a good lot of stockins knit again I get home again*

The pilot leaves in half an hour so good bye God bless you all

Sode Hanson

The *Picayune* arrived in Cronstadt, sometimes spelled Kronshtadt,
Russia on May 24, 1858. Cronstadt is on an island 16 miles off St. Petersburg in the Gulf of Finland. Tsar Peter the Great seized the Kotlin Island
in 1703. Here he built a fortress to protect shipping access to the port of
St. Petersburg. The island, surrounded by water only eight feet deep, was
and is so flat you do not see it on approach from the water. A narrow
winding channel, 26 to 28 feet deep serviced the port. The port was not
accessible six months of the year.

In his book *Russia of the Tsars*, James E. Strickler described why coun-
tries traded with Russia. After the War of 1812 with France, the soldiers
who fought had become aware that peasants from other areas could do
some reading and marketing. They returned to Russia with this concept
and began creating a little more than they needed of products like boots,
clothes, candles, and tools. They established markets, in larger cities, for
these goods. Slowly a demand for their goods exceeded their handwork
production, and merchants invested in machinery like power looms. The
merchants acquired a loom and hired and trained factory workers, but
they needed cotton, which had to be imported. Between 1825 and 1860,
during the Russian Industrial Revolution, Russian factories increased
their number of employees from 200,000 to 550,000. From 1830 to 1840,
Russia entered the grain export trade and sent ever increasing loads of
wheat, rye, and other grains, to the rapidly growing cities of Europe.

In 1855, when Alexander II came to power, he freed the serfs. It took six years for this freedom to be accomplished, but the serfs found work in the factories which provided the work force Russia needed to become an industrial nation.

About the time of Solon's letter from Dover, Frederic Echenagucia sent his sister-in-law a letter with an inquiry of the name of the vessel that Solon has taken to Russia. Francisco had a sister named Leen, and three brothers: Frederico, Herman, and Anton. Frederic maintained contact with Lucy Jane for many years after the death of his brother, Francisco, and took great interest in his nephew Herman. Frederic wrote his May 18, 1858 letter from St. Thomas. He had recently passed a Castine vessel near Pt. Plata but was not able to stop for communication with the Captain. His letter went by way of Havana to New York and finally to Castine.

DATED MAY 18, 1858, THIS LETTER FROM FREDERICK, THE BROTHER OF FRANCIS ECHANAGUCIA, TO LUCY JANE IN PENOBSCOT, MAINE, EXPRESSED HIS COMMITTMENT TO REMAIN IN CONTACT WITH HER.

St Thomas 18th May 1858

My Dear and remembered Sissy

Your kind and esteemed letter of the 28th of March last has reached me this morning by a schooner arrived from La Guavia. It is really a happy day for me, because I was so long on the lookout for a few of your lines; I had such an impression of joy by seeing your handwriting that I had to keep your letters for a few hours before taking notice of its contents.—I don't doubt about your astonishment for not receiving my news for so long a time; I thought that by my last written to you (last year) I had warned you that I intended to leave this place on a short trip to St Domingo Island, which i did; but unfortunately the revolution broke out on the 7th of July and by that reason I had to remain to that awful place till now 17 days ago.—everything went on very bad with me down there, but truly not with me alone; every one has suffered and many are yet suffering; all kind of trade is paralized and commerce is entirely at a standstill. The two belligerant parties are yet fighting each other, and a strict blockade has commenced a fortnight ago; happily we have not been caught by either of the party's vessels.—all these reasons will show you that, first; I have not been sick thank God, and second: that

I am far from being tired of writing to my Yankee sister as you say—you must not believe that my friendship is so short; all on the contrary, it has no end; and believe Sissy that I have great pleasure in receiving and answering your letters which are always so kind to me—I long to be able to go about your place and to visit all you; it is my warm wish to make acquaintance to your family who has been so good towards my dear brother Francois, and to kiss that little fellow and wicked Hermy who is so dear to me.—I tell you Sissy, that if that little boy takes after his father you will have the wickest of boys; for Francois was like quicksilver; and self when he was asleep yet he could not be quiet half a minute.—Herman has promised you his miniature and I think that I did also; I will try to send it to you by first good opportunity.—Herman has your's that I lend him, and he wont send it back to me.—When you write me again let me know the name of the vessel by which Solon has gone to Russia.

Leaving Pt. Plata the other day we pass near a vessel from Castine, and I assure you I was very sorry we could not stop a little to talk with the Captain, and to have given him a letter for you.—I would like very much to meet with some one going about your place to send some trifle or the other for my boy Hermy.—Yesterday I have received letters from Herman they are all well, except his wife Carmelita, who is a little indisposed in Caracas.

Anton is the onliest one of the brothers that never writes any one—Leen tells me that she has often attempted to write you, but she could not go on, because she has forgotten the English language, and also that her four children begin to break the paper and to pull down the inkstand, they are too wicked.

My best respects to our dear father and rest of the family, while I remain dear Sissy your affectionate brother.

Frederic

*Sissy, this letter goes by
the way of Havanna, I hope
it will reach you in short.—
If you write, direct your
letter to Mess.rs Moller & Riava of New York
                26 South Street
and they will forward it to me quite safe. Adieu*

I suffered like the devil in that cold snap for we have no stove in the forecastle and was at work in the water almost all the time and it would freeze any where but things are a little better now we have a first rate stove in the forecastle and the weather is quite moderate.

we have got the dog again and pa has concluded to bring him home he is such a prime handy critter about the ship I stopped at capt Eatons all night when I was in castine dad is going to give me her dog type when I get back that is rich

I have not recieved any letter from jed Freathy yet and I dont know what to make of it I should thought he would wrote.

Give my love to all the boys or girls that think enough about me to inquire about me. tell Hoxie that we wish he was here for we have only two for a crew I shall try to get this letter in the office to day if I can I dont suppose it will be of any use to answer this I have not recieved any answer to the other one yet. Give my love to Lucy Jane Anne and Henry and save a large piece for yourself. having no more room I shall have to close so good bye

Solon Hanson himself

One of Solon Hanson's letters

Chapter 12

SOLON'S FINAL VOYAGE

S OLON'S FINAL VOYAGE is described in a single letter from Captain John Brooks. Solon's diary was preserved with his letters, and years later the blank pages were used by his father to keep some farm accounts. Lucy Jane's family Bible has been passed down for several generations. She recorded in it the following:

> Solon J. Hanson died in
> Cronstadt Russia
> July 10th 1858 aged 19 years and 11 months
> "Let not your hearts be troubled ye believe in God
> Believe also in me."

From Lucy Jane's Bible, the well marked Psalm 107, Verses 23–31, is reprinted here.

> *They that go down to the sea in ships,*
> *that do business in the great waters,*
> *these see the works of the Lord,*
> *and his wonders in the deep.*
> *For he commandeth and raiseth the stormy wind,*
> *which lifteth up the waves thereof.*
> *They mount up to the heavens,*
> *they go down again to the depths:*
> *their soul is melted because of trouble*
> *They reel to and fro, and stagger like a drunken man,*
> *and are at their wits' end.*

Then they cry unto the Lord in their trouble,
  and he bringeth them out of their distresses.
He maketh the storm a calm,
  so that the waves thereof are still.
Then are they glad because they are quiet;
  so he bringeth them unto their desired haven.
Oh, that men would praise the Lord for his goodness,
  and for his wonderful works
  to the children of men!

A handwritten song-poem was also in that Bible. Sheet music published in 1909 for a ballad called "Anchored" had similar lyrics written by Samuel K. Cowan and music by Michael Watson.

Flying, with flowing sail,
  Over the Summer sea!
Sheer thro the seething gale
  Homeward bound was She! . . .
Flying with feathery prow.
Bounding with slanting keel . . .
And glad . . . and glad was the sailor lad,
As he steer'd . . . and sang at his wheel.

Chorus
Only another day to stray . . .
Only another night to warm
Then safe . . . at last the harbor past
Safe in my fathers home
  Safe in my fathers home

Bright on the flashing brine,
Glit-tered the summer sun!
Sweetly the star-ry shone
Smile when the day is done!
Blithe was the breeze of Heav'n,
Filling the flying sail, . . .

And glad was the sailor lad,
So he sterr'd and sang thro' the gale

Chorus

Sud-den the light-ning flash'd
Like fal-chims in the dark!
Sud-den the thun-ders crash'd!
Alas for the gal-lent bark!
The storm had pass'd
A drea-ry wreck lay she!
And a soft smile came from the stars,
And a voice from the whispering foam
Safe at last the danger past
Safe in his Fathers home
Safe in his Fathers home

A LETTER FROM CAPTAIN JOHN BROOKS REPORTS SOLON'S DEATH TO HIS
FAMILY. CAPTAIN BROOKS WROTE THE LETTER IN CRONSTADT ON JULY 13,
1858.

Cronstadt July 13, 1858

Capt John Hanson

Dear Sir

*I set down to day to perform a painful duty. The "Picayune" has been in
port six weeks and is now nearly nearly loaded for Bristol. Eng. Everything
went on well until last week when your son Solon was taken sick. Thursday. the 8th he was about his work as usual. in the Afternoon he told Mr.
Wescott he had the diarrhea and he gave him some cholrea* [cholera] *drops
to stop it. The next morning he was no better. but was able to set about
decks under the awning until evening when he became worse. and the mate
went after the Doctor. who came on board and recomended sending him to
the Hospital. which was done about 8 oclock in the evening. Friday. Two of
the boys set up with him that night. He was taken about ten with violent
cramps. and all the symptoms of the cholrea. Although everything was done
for him that was possible the cramps continued until the next forenoon*

Saturday the 10th. About ten oclock the cramps left him and he was free from pain. and became aware that he did not have long to live. Henry Stover was with him at the time. and will write the particulars of what he said and done in his last moments. He passed away calmly and quietly at half past one o clock. Saturday. We were all much grieved as much as if he had been a brother. He was a favorite with all on board the ship. And there is not one in the ship whose death would have been so keenly felt. "Poor fellow," he was so good here. I know he must be happy where he is. There is fifteen American Ships in Port. and it seems strange that he should be taken the first one. with the awful discease. It is generally the case. the best are taken away. while some poor miserable being will live for years. They say such things happen for the best. but it hardly seems so to me sometimes. Perhaps the one that is taken away is better off. but it is awful for those that are left behind. I knew that change generally had a bad effect especialy in hot weather. So as soon as I arrived here I procured a large bottle of medicine for the diarrhea and told Mr. Wescott to take charge of it and keep a look out for the boys and give it to them as soon as they complained in the least. I am afraid Solon was rather imprudent when he was first taken with the dysentery. After he was taken to the Hospital. I learned from the other boys that he eat a whole bottle of milk with bread the night before. Thursday. I have since learned from Doctor that milk is the very worst thing a person can take under such circumstances. So while poor Solon was doing what he thought was for the best. it was the worst. thing he could have done. He went to bed with the milk on his stomach and in the morning was much worse. Mr. Wescott wanted to go for the Doctor that morning. but Solon did not think much ailed him and was against sending. It is hard. very hard. for you all at home but I suppose it was ordained so to be. We all attended the funeral yesterday at the English Church and followed the remains to the English burying ground. The case was so sudden that I can hardly realise that the poor boy is no more. I do not know when I seen a finer young man than he was. always in good humor and good spirits rain or shine he was always smiling. I know he must be happy wherever he is. He was so stout and healthy I never once dreamed of his being taken away. The ways of the Lord are truly mysteriory. I have been to day. and ordered a grave stone. with name birth place age & I have had is clothes packed up just as he left them. the day before he died. and will send them to Boston. care of Martin

L. Hal [illegible] *in the ship "Harry Bluff." Capt Redman. who will leave here in a few weeks.*

Yours Respectfully John H. Brooks

THE

MARINER'S
MEDICAL GUIDE;

DESIGNED FOR THE USE OF

Ships, Families, and Plantations.

CONTAINING THE

SYMPTOMS AND TREATMENT OF DISEASES.

ALSO,

A LIST OF MEDICINES, THEIR USES, AND THE MODE OF
ADMINISTERING, WHEN A PHYSICIAN
CANNOT BE PROCURED.

———

Selected from Standard Works.

———

BY JAMES FOLSOM.

FIFTH EDITION, REVISED.

BOSTON:
PUBLISHED BY JAMES FOLSOM,
209 COMMERCIAL ST., AND 1 EASTERN AVENUE.

1874.

Cholera Morbus.

SYMPTOMS. — This complaint generally comes on very suddenly. It usually commences with nausea and pain in the stomach, followed by severe griping and distress in the abdomen. These symptoms are immediately succeeded by vomiting and purging, which generally continue in paroxysms until great prostration follows.

TREATMENT. — Give several draughts of warm water, flaxseed tea or rice water, at the commencement of vomiting and purging, in order to remove all the solid contents of the stomach and bowels; apply hot mustard seed poultices over the pit of the stomach. After making use of the above, take one tea-spoonful Bi Carb. Soda, (No. 8,) or saleratus, one tea-spoonful, Powdered Rhubarb, (No. 45,) two tea-spoonfuls; one tea-spoonful cayenne, or two of ginger; essence of peppermint, half a wineglass; warm water, half a pint, and take a table-spoonful every hour until the evacuations show an improved appearance, when the dose may be diminished. If the bowels continue relaxed, add a few drops Laudanum, (No. 16,) to each dose. The cause of this complaint is exposure to extreme heat, and sudden checking of perspiration. Also unripe fruit, shell fish, &c.

Asiatic Cholera.

SYMPTOMS. — This disease when fully established is almost invariably fatal. It generally commences with a diarrhœa, accompanied with little or no pain; this may continue for three or four days, but often only for a few

6 *

Timeline

1814
End of the War of 1812 with the Treaty of Ghent.

1820
Maine admitted to the Union as the 23rd state.
Elizabeth Peabody established the first organized kindergarten,
in Lancaster Mass.

1821
Maine established its first and the nation's second free high school in Portland.

1825
Erie Canal connecting the Great Lakes with the Hudson River completed.
"Portrait of Gilbert Stuart," painting by Sarah Goodridge.
Birth of Johann Strauss Jr. who wrote *The Blue Danube Waltz*.

1826
Birth of Stephen Foster.

1830
News dispatches from Europe arrived in 3 months by sail.
Baltimore and Ohio railroad opened 13 miles of railroad track.

1833
Birth of Johannes Brahms.

1835
"Roseate Spoonbill," painting by John James Audubon.

1837
The newspaper *The New Orleans Picayune* is founded.
Victoria became Queen of Great Britain and Ireland. She ruled until 1901.

1839
Charles Goodyear accidentally discovers the process of vulcanization.
The daguerreotype is introduced.
The Voyage of the Beagle by Charles Darwin.
Birth of Anna Eliza Hardy, itinerant portrait/landscape painter, Bangor, Maine.

1840
Penny Post introduced in England by Roland Hill.
Two Years Before the Mast by Richard Henry Dana.
"Moonlight, Nagakubo," painting by Ando Hiroshige.

1841

John Hampton receives a patent for Venetian blinds.
The Deerslayer by James Fenimore Cooper.
Birth of children's book illustrator, Kate Greenaway.

1842

Completion of the Bunker Hill Monument in Boston. This was the
first Patriotic monument begun in 1825.
Faberge firm founded by Gusten Faberge in St. Petersburg, Russia.
Haviland China company established in Limoges, France.
The Webster-Asburton Treaty settles the boundary with
Canada along the Atlantic coast to the St. Lawrence.

1843

A Christmas Carol by Charles Dickens.

1844

Experimental telegraph line between Washington and Baltimore by
Professor S. F. B. Morse with money appropriated by Congress.
The Count of Monte Cristo by Alexander Dumas, the father.

1845

"Fur Traders Descending the Missouri," painting by George Caleb Bingham.

1846

Northwest Boundary set at 49°.
Failure of the potato crop in Ireland.
Congress organized The Smithsonian Institution at Washington, D.C. with startup
money from the estate of English chemist and philanthropist James Smithson.

1847

Commercial panic in Europe.
Henry David Thoreau climbed Mt. Katahdin, then wrote *The Maine Woods*.
Jane Eyre by Charlotte Bronte.
Omoo by Herman Melville.
Death of John Chapman, known as Johnny Appleseed.
1846–1848 War with Mexico secures Texas for the United States.

1848

Discovery of gold in California.
Rev. Jonathan Fisher, of Blue Hill Maine, copied his 1824 self-
portrait three times so each daughter could have one.
"State of Maine Pure Spruce Gum" made in Bangor Maine.

1849
The Oregon Trail by Francis Parkman.

1850
Maine had a population of 583,169.
"View of Castine, Maine," painting by Fitz Hugh Lane.

1851
Maine Law passed to prohibit the manufacture of alcohol and its sale in the state.
The first Great World's Fair Exhibition held in London.
The House of Seven Gables by Nathaniel Hawthorne.
"Mount Desert," painting by Frederic E. Church.

1852
Uncle Tom's Cabin by Harriet Beecher Stowe.

1853
The three years of yellow fever epidemics begin. 11,000 people die of the disease.

1854
Treaty with Japan for commercial ventures negotiated by Commodore Peary.
"Bonjour, Monsieur Corbet," painting by Gustave Corbet.
Ellsworth American newspaper began publication.

1855
Westward Ho! By Charles Kingsley.

1851–1856
Yellow Fever begins in South America and spreads north, reaching New York. Lack of sanitation thought to be the cause. The winters were mild with warm springs followed by intense heat in the summer. Everything remained damp, moulds grew everywhere. The mortality rates were very high.

1857
The first nighttime torchlight procession is held during the Mardi Gras.
Financial crash; many businesses do not survive.
The Gleaners by Jean-Francois Millet.

1858
First cable laid across the Atlantic Ocean from Trinity Bay, Newfoundland to Valentia Bay, Ireland. The cable was 1,640 miles in length.
The eraser was added to the pencil.
The Courtship of Miles Standish by Henry Wadsworth Longfellow.
"Packing the Catch," pastel by William P. Stubbs, Bucksport artist.

Bibliography

American Boy's Book of Sports and Games. New York: Dick & Fitzgerald, 1864.

Anonymous. *Observations and Instructions for the use of the Commissioned, the Junior and Other Officers of the Royal Navy, on all Material Points of Professional Duty.* London: P. Steel, 1804, second edition 1807, third edition, 1841.

Belanger, Pamela J. *Maine America: American Art at the Farnsworth Art Museum.* Published by The Farnsworth Museum of Art, Rockland Maine.

Bowditch, Nathaniel. *American Practical Navigator.* Washington: United States Hydrographic Office, U.S. Government Publishing Office, 1939.

Burns, Robert. *The Poetical Works of Robert Burns.* Boston: Phillips, Sampson and Company, 1856.

Carse, Robert. *The Twilight of Sailing Ships.* New York: Galahad Books.

Castine Historical Society. *Images of America: Castine.* Arcadia Publishing. 1996.

Castine Visitor. Spring 1998

Chase, Mary Ellen. *Jonathan Fisher Maine Parson, 1769–1847.* New York: The Macmillan Company. 1948.

Collier, Sargent F. *Down East Maine: Prince Edward Island, Nova Scotia, The Gaspe.* Boston: Houghton Mifflin Company, 1953.

Dana, Richard, *Two Years Before the Mast,* 1832.

Doudiet, Ellenore. *Majabigwaduce: Castine. Penobscot. Brooksville.* Castine, Maine: Castine Scientific Society, 1978.

Druett, Joan. *Hen Frigates: Wives of Merchant Captains Under Sail.* New York: Simon & Schuster, 1998.

Duncan, Roger. *Coastal Maine: A Maritime History.* New York: W. W. Norton, 1992.

Filisky, Michael. *Peterson First Guides: Fishes of North America.* Houghton Mifflin Company, 1989.

Griffiths, John Anslem. *Observations on Some Points of Seamanship: with Practical Hints on Naval Oeconomy, &c.* (1st). Cheltenham: J. J. Hadley, 1824.

———. *The U.S. Nautical Magazine,* Vol. III (1855–56), page 344.

———. *The U.S. Nautical Magazine,* Vol. V, (Oct. 1856), page 66–69.

Griffith's Ship Builder's Manual, 1856.

Harper's New Monthly Magazine. Vol. XV, June to November 1857. New York: Harper & Brothers Publisher, 1857.

Honey, Mark. *Abigail & Sarah Hawes of Castine: Navigators and Educators.* Lois Moore Cyr, editor, 1996.

———. *The Leaches of Penobscot: Part VI: Sea Captains of Penobscot.* Self-published by Mark Honey, October, 1997.

————. "Standing Before the Mast," articles in the *Castine Patriot*, 1999.

Hutchins, Jack Randolph. *Hugh Hutchins of Old England,* including book *Enoch Hutchings of Kittery* by Richard Jasper Hutchings. Gateway Press, Inc., 1984.

Ives, Edward. "Amos Hanson, Fisherman: Poet of the Bagaduce." Talk given at Wilson Museum, August, 1998.

Kipping, Robert. *The Elements Treatise on Sails and Sailmaking: A Dictionary of Technical Terms Relative to Sails,* Weale's Rudimentary Series, no. 149, 1847. Transcribed by Lars Bruzelius (http://www.bruzelius.info/Nautica/Etymology/English/Kipping(1847).html).

Mitchell, Frederick, *Penobscot Bicentennial: 1787–1987* published by the Penobscot Historical Society, 1987.

Myers, Albert E. "The Hutchins Family of Penobscot Maine," 1996. "A Family of the Bagaduce," Harrisburg, Penn., 1976.

National Archives. Records of the Bureau of Customs (record group 36), Collection of District Records Coastwise Manifest.

O'Leary, Wayne M. *Maine Sea Fisheries: the Rise and Fall of a Native Industry, 1830–1890.* Northeastern University Press, 1996.

"Our Fishing Heritage." Video by Minotaur productions on vessel fishing.

Paine, Lincoln P. *Down East: A Maritime History of Maine.* Gardiner, Maine: Tilbury House Publishers, 2000.

Reader's Digest Guide to Places of the World: A Geographical Dictionary. Reader's Digest, 1995.

Ridpath, John Clark. *A Popular History of the United States of America.* Cincinnati-Memphis-Philadelphia-Chicago-Atlanta: A. M. Jones Brothers & Co., 1876.

Rowe, William Hutchinson, *The Maritime History of Maine: Three Centuries of Shipbuilding and Seafaring,* New York: W. W. Norton and Company, 1948.

Royce, Patrick. *Royce's Sailing Illustrated.* Valencia, Calif.: Delta Lithograph, 1993.

Speare, M. E. *Pocket Book of Verse,* Collectors edition, Pocket Books, Inc., New York,1940.

Stoddard, John L. *John L. Stoddard's Lectures.* Vol. VI. Boston: Balch Brothers Co., 1898.

Strickler, James E. *Russia of the Tsars.* Lucent Books, 1998.

Swain, Ruth Freeman. *How Sweet It is (and Was): The History of Candy.* New York: Holiday House, 2003.

Taylor, Henry. *Instructions for Mariners Respecting the Management of Ships at Single Anchor, and General Rules for Sailing; Also Directions for Crossing the North Sea, the Cattegat, &c.* (7th) First edition 1792. London: James Imray and Son, 1861.

Wasson, George S. *Sailing Down on the Penobscot: The Story of the River and the Bay in the Old Days,* new ed. New York: W.W. Norton, 1949.

Wheeler, George A., assisted by Louise Wheeler Bartlett. *History of Castine Penobscot and Brooksville, Maine.* Privately printed Cornwall, New York, 1923.

Wilson Museum Bulletin, Castine, Maine. Winter, 1984.

Woodard, Colin. *The Lobster Coast: Rebels, Rusticators, and the Struggle for a Forgotten Frontier*. New York: Viking Penguin Group, 2004.

Woodward, James. *The Sea-Man's Vade Mecum*. London, 1707. Transcribed by Lars Bruzelius (http://www.bruzelius.info/nautica/Etymology/English/x707Seam.html).

World Book Encyclopedia. (Volume C–CH and volume P). Field Enterprises Educational Corporation, 1965.

Index

Adams (Ship) 47, 95–97, 102, 103, 107, 112, 114
Adams, Samuel 102
Albion (Ship) 78, 82, 84
American Maritime Heritage 49
Anderson, John 99
Andrews, William 95, 102
Atherton, Mrs. 18
Avery, Captain Thatcher 7
Avery, Isiah 18
Bagaduce 1, 34, 43, 137
bark 57, 58, 61, 63, 65, 93, 97
barkentine 57
Bass. Esq., J. H. 63
Bok, Gordon 16
Bowditch, Nathaniel 28
Brewster, Captain 82
Bridges, Bill 91
Bridges, Dan 25
Bridges, George 90
Bridges, Josh 121
brig 9, 55, 56, 60, 62, 111
brigantine 56
Brooks, Captain John H. 87, 88, 90, 127, 129, 131
Brown, J. Ross 49
Bryant, C. 62
Bryant, Mr. 9
Bucksport Herald 59
Cadiz (Spain) 61, 62, 64, 104
Canso 44, 45
Cape Cod 77
Captains
   Avery, Thatcher 7
   Brewster 82
   Brooks, John H. 87, 88, 90, 100, 127, 129, 131
   Bryant, C. 62
   Chase 67, 72, 92
   Cornwallis 62
   Devereux 116
   Dunbar 7
   Eaton 53, 62
   Echenagucia, Francisco 43, 45, 55, 56, 58, 60, 61, 63, 64–65
   Gardner, John 62
   Gray 8, 9, 90, 92, 107, 110, 112, 114

Hanson, Amos 7, 8, 16, 18, 25–27, 33, 41, 43, 96, 97, 105, 112, 114, 137
Hanson, James 22
Hanson, John 5–10, 12, 13, 15, 16–19, 20, 24, 27, 33, 43, 44–45, 55, 64, 65, 115, 129
Jerry 46
Leach family 24
Lucy 82
Lufkin 71
Mullet 45, 62
Perkins, Joseph 5, 43, 50, 61, 63–65, 78, 91
Peterson, John Foster 58
Redman 131
Simpson 93
Thompson, Jim 82, 84
Wardwell 82
Castine ix, 1–3, 5–10, 12, 15–17, 19, 20, 23, 25, 27, 28, 34, 35, 43–48, 50, 53, 58, 61, 63–66, 77–80, 84, 87, 88, 90, 92, 96, 102–106, 114, 115, 121, 123, 124, 135–137
Castine (Ship) 87, 90, 93, 98, 100–104, 106, 114
Castine-Penobscot Maine region ix
Castine Town Hall 7
Cate, Mr. 52
Chase, Captain 67, 72, 92
Chase, Frank 73
Cherryfield 49, 55, 56, 60, 62
Civil War 6, 58, 80, 109
Closson, Hiram 75
cod xi, 6, 40, 46–48, 59, 77, 79–81, 87, 102, 105
Conner, Edwin Solon 35, 58, 79
Conner, Everett 58
Conner, Fred Morton 58
Conner, Helen Peterson ix, 1
Conner, John 106, 116
Conner, Vivian Kenniston ix
Connor, Eb 93, 106, 112, 114
Cornwallis, Captain 62
Daggett, Kendrick 67, 68, 136
Dana, Richard 36, 37
Desisle, Mr. J. B. 116
Devereux, Captain 18
Devereux, Charley 116

THIS BOOK AND OTHER FINE BOOKS ABOUT
NEW ENGLAND MAY BE ORDERED AT:
WWW.HOBBLEBUSH.COM